FEARLESS AND FREE

Other books by George Walton:

THE WASTED GENERATION
LET'S END THE DRAFT MESS
FAINT THE TRUMPET SOUNDS
TWELVE EVENTS THAT CHANGED OUR WORLD
THE TARNISHED SHIELD
SENTINEL OF THE PLAINS
CAPTAIN MADAM

Co-author of:

THE DEVIL'S BRIGADE
ROME FELL TODAY
THE CHAMPAIGN CAMPAIGN

FEARLESS AND FREE

The Seminole Indian War
1835–1842

BY

GEORGE WALTON

THE BOBBS-MERRILL COMPANY, INC.

Indianapolis/New York

Designed by Jacques Chazaud
Manufactured in the United States of America

First printing

Library of Congress Cataloging in Publication Data

Walton, George H.
  Fearless and free.

  Bibliography: p.
  Includes index.
  1. Seminole War, 2d, 1835–1842. I. Title.
E83.835.W33   973.5'7   76-11616
ISBN 0-672-52250-0

For Virginia

Acknowledgments

An historical work of this type cannot be the result of the author's effort alone. It is the combined production of many persons, living and dead.

My deep appreciation goes to Professor John K. Mahon, Chairman of the History Department at the University of Florida; Sara D. Jackson of the National Archives, Consultant to the Department of History of Howard University; Dean Virginia Walton Hodges of Georgia Southern College; Camilla Hannon, Reference Librarian of the National Archives; Mary Johnson, formerly of the National Archives; Doctor Gustave Harrer, Director of the Libraries of the University of Florida; Josephine Motylewski of the National Archives; Jeanne Billingsley, Librarian of the Cedar Key Branch of the Central Florida Regional Library, Ocala; and William Sartain of the Library of Congress; who all contributed materially to this effort.

Louis and Dolores McGuinness made available their farm, Lord Fairfax's Hunting Lodge, at Cedar Grove, Virginia, where most of this book was written. Without their encouragement, their editorial assistance, and their suggestions, this book would not have seen the light of day.

The painstaking attention to detail of Linda B. Webb, who typed, and Mary Frances Haynes, who read the manuscript, went far above and beyond the call of duty. They have my thanks.

To these and the many others who contributed goes my heartfelt appreciation.

GEORGE WALTON

Cedar Keys, Florida
January 4, 1975

Contents

FEARLESS AND FREE

The whites . . . dealt unjustly by me. I came to them, they deceived me; the land I was upon I loved, my body is made of its sands; the Great Spirit gave me legs to walk over it; hands to aid myself; eyes to see its ponds, rivers, forests, and game; then a head with which I think. The sun, which is warm and bright as my feelings are now, shines to warm us and bring forth our crops, and the moon brings back the spirit of our warriors, our fathers, wives, and children. The white man comes; he grows pale and sick, why cannot we live here in peace? I have said I am the enemy to the white man. I could live in peace with him, but they first steal our cattle and horses, cheat us, and take our lands. The white men are as thick as the leaves in the hammocks; they come upon us thicker every year. They may shoot us, drive our women and children night and day; they may chain our hands and feet, but the red man's heart will be always free.

—A SEMINOLE INDIAN CHIEF

CHAPTER I

Murder and Massacre- Christmas 1835

War at best is barbarism.

WILLIAM TECUMSEH SHERMAN

Brevet Major Francis Langhorn Dade, a veteran of the War of 1812, a prudent and able officer, arrived at Fort Brooke on December 21, 1835.

A native Virginian, he was born on the anniversary of Washington's birthday in 1792, on the family plantation overlooking the Potomac River in King George County, where his great-grandfather had settled in 1645.

As a youth Dade led the typical life of the son of a well-to-do country family. A private tutor, hunting, fishing and riding were part of his daily routine until he became of age, when his father secured him a direct commission in the army as a 3rd lieutenant in the Twelfth Infantry Regiment.

The War of 1812 was in progress, and Dade saw combat. He became a 2nd lieutenant in 1814 and was later transferred to the Fourth Infantry. He became a 1st lieutenant in 1816 and a captain in 1818.

Following Spain's ratification of the treaty ceding Florida to the United States in 1821, the Fourth Infantry Regiment was transferred to the new Territory, and there Dade was to spend the remainder of his life. In 1828 Dade was breveted a major for ten years of faithful service in one grade.*

Dade learned that considerable apprehension was felt for the garrison at Fort King, a post in Central Florida "on the southern border of Alachua," the territory designated for the Seminole Indians.

No word had been received from Lieutenant Colonel Alexander C. W. Fanning, its commander, in over a month. A fiery little one-armed Yankee, Fanning, a West Pointer, was not the sort who would fail to report his situation. When Key West had last heard from him his garrison was down to a strength of but forty-six men, and both ammunition and other supplies were low.

When Dade arrived at Fort Brooke, commanded by Captain Francis Belton, an expedition for the relief of Fort King was already in preparation, under the command of Captain George Washington Gardiner, brother-in-law of Colonel Fanning. Dade, however, having a brevet majority, assumed command of the Fort King relief expedition, a detachment of 108 men.

The Negro slave Louis Pacheco was sent along as a guide and interpreter for the force. He had been leased to the Army for twenty-five dollars a month. He not only knew the country through which the troops would pass but also spoke several of the Seminole dialects.

During the first day's march there seemed little likelihood that the command would be attacked so near the fort, but Major

* A brevet was a commission promoting an officer to a higher rank than that which he held by virtue of his commission in a particular unit. The brevet, given for bravery or meritorious service, provided no increase in pay and limited the exercise of the higher rank.[1]

Dade took every precaution. An advance guard preceded the troops, and flankers were put out. By mid-afternoon they were within sight of the Little Hillsborough. Dade stopped his men and set them to felling trees and constructing a small barricade around their entire bivouac area.

Four oxen had proven inadequate to the task of pulling the six-pounder, and the forward movement of the column had been tied to their slow pace. A conference of the officers resulted in the gun being temporarily abandoned. On the evening of the 23rd, Lieutenant Benjamin Alvord was sent back to Fort Brooke with the request that horses be sent forward to pick up the gun and bring it to the expedition.

As the relief force had more officers than necessary, Alvord, a young man of twenty-two, was directed not to return. His remaining at the post would save his life. Before daybreak of the 24th, three enlisted men with extra horses from the fort picked up the six-pounder and brought it forward. They returned to Brooke the next morning.

Reveille sounded before first light on the 24th. Before the first pink signs of day could be detected in the east the troops of the relief force were well on their way.

In the late morning the column passed the cypress-studded Lake Thlonotosassa, near which was buried the body of Private Kinsley H. Dalton of the Third Regiment, a mail courier who, only the previous August, had been killed by Indians on his way to Fort Brooke.

By five o'clock the troops had reached the south bank of the Big Hillsborough River. Nearby they found the fire-gutted foundations of the house of William Saunders, a trader.

All that remained of the bridge that for eleven years had spanned the river were a few charred logs. On a high bluff the troopers built a stockade and there made their Christmas Eve camp. Major Dade knew fording the river would take at least half a day, during which time the troops would be vulnerable to Seminole attack. If the Indians planned to strike, this would be the most propitious time.

At Fort Brooke, Dade had learned that Major John Mountford was on his way to the post by transport from Pensacola, with two companies totaling about a hundred men. Dade had been promised that upon their arrival at the fort, Mountford and his men would be sent forward to join the Fort King relief force. Major Dade accordingly asked for volunteers to take a message back to Captain Belton. A twenty-four-year-old blond New Englander, Private Aaron Jewell, stepped forward.

Jewell, filled with visions of glamour and glory, had enlisted in the army, but had found the life not up to his expectations. The previous January, with a little over two years of his enlistment to go, he had gone AWOL. Now, by volunteering for a dangerous mission, he was hoping to expunge his previous bad conduct from his record.

Jewell was to tell Captain Belton that the bridge over the Big Hillsborough had been destroyed and was not repairable, and that Major Mountford, if he had arrived, was to be sent north as rapidly as possible with his two companies and his extra supplies and ammunition.

With the help of one of the less exhausted horses, Jewell reached Fort Brooke a little after midnight. He delivered his message to Captain Belton, but was told that Major Mountford had not yet arrived. After a short sleep, Private Jewell voluntarily returned north for no other apparent reason than to be with the men of his company on Christmas Day.

Jewell had hardly left on his return trip when Major Mountford's transport was sighted. Unfortunately, half of his men were in a second transport, which did not arrive until the following day, and all the baggage, equipment, and supplies were in a third ship. The latter vessel had run aground, and all

4

plans for a meeting of the two forces were accordingly abandoned.

By noon Dade's men had crossed the river, and in wet, cold, flapping uniforms they continued to plod north. They passed several ponds and a lake, and in the late afternoon, some ten miles short of the Withlacoochee River, the expedition bivouacked for the night. Again they felled trees and threw up a crude breastwork.

Following their meager supper, they greeted Private Jewell on his return from the mission to Fort Brooke. He was wildly acclaimed, and there was no question but that his fellow soldiers, whom he wished to be with on Christmas, admired his courage.

On Saturday the 26th the relief force arrived at the Withlacoochee. All that remained of the bridge spanning the river were gaunt, blackened pilings. The stream was only twenty feet in width, and trees were soon felled to allow a dry crossing for the men. The officers on horseback, the wagons, and even the caisson were soon across the creek.

A mile beyond the burned bridge they passed a deserted Seminole village. It seemed peaceful, but in its very silence there was menace. They pushed on. That night, a few miles above the Little Withlacoochee, the troops once more surrounded their bivouac area with a log stockade.

Unbeknownst to Dade, the progress of his command had been carefully followed by the Seminole and their Negro allies. Plans had been made to attack the relief expedition as it crossed the Hillsborough River and later the Little Withlacoochee but had been canceled at the last minute by the principal Chief, Micanopy, and his Chancellor, Abraham.

Micanopy, whose name was compounded of the Seminole words *Mico,* a chief, and *annuppa,* topmost, was a descendant of Cowcatcher, of the original Alachua band, who is generally credited with being the founder of the Seminole Nation.

5

Mick-E-No-Pah, First Chief of the Tribe,
by George Catlin, 1837

Micanopy's five-foot-six frame managed to support his 300 pounds, but his walk resembled a waddling duck's. Although he was only thirty-five at the start of the Seminole War, self-indulgence and an ungovernable appetite had aged Micanopy. Strangers who met him thought he was in his late fifties or early sixties. General Duncan L. Clinch wrote that Micanopy was "a man of but little talent or energy of character." However, he was not completely stupid or dull; rather he was gullible and easily influenced by the person with whom he had last spoken.

That person was generally his Chancellor, Abraham.

The reason for the failure of the Indians and the Negroes to attack Major Dade's troops at the crossing of the Hillsborough River and at the Little Withlacoochee was not simply procrastination on the part of Micanopy and Abraham. They were awaiting the return of their War Chieftain, Osceola,* who was on a mission in the vicinity of Fort King, a mission he had been planning for almost a year.

Osceola has been described as short, slight, and round-shouldered, with small hands and feet. His forehead was high and "cast in an intellectual mold . . . the upper portion . . . was generally concealed by his hair being worn low and hanging out in front . . ."[4] His black eyes were deep and restless, giv-

---

* Osceola, born about 1800, probably among the Creek Indians on the Tallapoosa River in Georgia, was called Powell by the whites, a name thought to be that of his Scottish father, grandfather, or stepfather. The name Osceola, under which he would become famous, was the white man's corruption of the Creek name Asi Yaholo, or "black drink singer," which he had been given as a youth. He himself always insisted that he was of pure Indian blood. George Catlin, who later painted his portrait, was of the opinion that Osceola represented a typical "full blood and wild Indian."[2] Mark F. Boyd, however, presents a quite convincing argument to the contrary.[3] It is just possible that the stories of his mixed blood are an invention of the whites of the day who refused to believe that an Indian without a Caucasian background could be as intelligent and able a warrior as was Osceola.

7

Osceola, the Black Drink, Distinguished Warrior,
by George Catlin

ing him generally a thoughtful appearance, but when aroused they were full of fire. Ironically, his rather pointed nose and finely chiseled lips tended to give him a pleasant, almost sweet, expression. His voice was high and shrill. Like most of his fellow Indians who attained manhood, he possessed extraordinary physical endurance and had the reputation of being a great hunter.

While no one has ever disputed his courage, contemporary white opinion was divided as to Osceola's character.*

Although hardly more than a boy, he had fought against the United States in 1814 during the War of 1812. In General Andrew Jackson's campaign of 1818, he again took up arms. Although he was eventually captured, he began to show the qualities of leadership that would later bring him national and even international fame.

Not having been born to high rank, Osceola had no claim to hereditary leadership. Gradually, however, he began to assume an important position among the Indians and by 1835 was the

---

* Jacob Rhett Motte, an army surgeon, wrote of him:

> . . . he was a ruling spirit among those wretches, and exercised with autocratic power the sway he had acquired by his superior shrewdness and sagacity over their stern minds, and exacted from them the homage of vassals and dependents. . . . Yet in consequence of being averse to murdering women and children and prisoners in cold blood, according to Indian custom, his popularity was in some measure considerably weakened. . . .[5]

Another Army surgeon, Nathan S. Jarvis, who observed Osceola during his captivity, reported that his "countenance was expressive of mildness and benevolence [and] devoid of any suggestion of fierceness or determination."[6] And Lieutenant W. W. Smith says that he ". . . combined the gallantry, cool courage and sagacity of the white and the ferocity, savage daring and subtlety of the Indian."[7] Woodburne Potter, however, speaks of Osceola as not possessing ". . . the nobler Indian characteristics, but [being] perverse and obstinate, exhibiting a low and sordid spirit which produced difficulties in intercourse," and says that "his talents were not above a mediocre level."[8]

acknowledged War Chief of the Seminole. He also became the principal and most outspoken opponent of the government's policy of western migration for the eastern Indians.

Not far from Osceola's village was Fort King,* which had been established in 1827 as a military post intended "to compel the Indians to remain within their limits and give protection and security to the citizens of Florida."[9] It was also the headquarters of Indian agent General Wiley Thompson.

A barricade measuring 162 by 152 feet was erected of split logs pointed at the ends and sunk into the ground. Gates, a fourteen-foot watch tower, and quarters were built. A kitchen, mess halls, an ammunition pit, and a blacksmith's shop filled the remainder of the space within the barricade.

About a hundred yards in front of the main gate stood the office of the Indian agent. As the war clouds gathered, Osceola became a frequent visitor at the agency, and he and the general became friends. Certainly the agent admired the Indian, calling him "one of the most bold, daring and intrepid chiefs of this [the Seminole] nation." Later General Thompson gave him an expensive rifle as a present.

Wiley Thompson, a Georgian, had obtained his military title

---

* Territorial Governor William P. DuVal for several years had urged the establishment of a military post "on the southern border of Alachua," the territory assigned to the Seminole, and in 1826 the War Department acquiesced. Captain James M. Glassell, with two companies of infantry, selected the site and made camp there on March 25, 1827. The post was originally called Camp or Cantonment King, in honor of Colonel William King of the Fourth Infantry, who had died the previous year.

It is not hard to determine the motives that led to the selection of the site of Fort King. "A large and beautiful spring" (originally discovered by Colonel Gad Humphreys, an Indian agent, in 1825) from which a deep creek led to the Ocklawaha River and thence to the St. Johns River and the Atlantic Ocean made water transportation possible and a long overland hauling of supplies unnecessary. The post, was located on an elevation, with good water available, amidst "a verdant growth of magnolias, hickories and other hardwoods."

by serving from 1817 to 1824 as a major general of that state's militia. Previously he had been with Andrew Jackson in the Creek War. At the time of his appointment as agent he was finishing his fifth term as a Georgia Representative in the United States Congress.

As early as January 1832, the Federal Government had determined to move all eastern Indians west of the Mississippi River. On October 21, 1834, Thompson called together the Seminole Chiefs and told them that the question was not *whether* they wanted to stay in Florida or move to the West but *how* migration was to be effected. That night the Chiefs held their own council, and Osceola, who had not been softened by his friendship with the agent or by the gift of the rifle, was not only able to intimidate many of his fellow leaders into opposing migration, but even proposed proscribing any Indian who favored the government policy. Consequently, further meetings with the agent accomplished nothing.

On March 27, 1835, at a session at Fort King during which the wooden platform on which the principal dignitaries were seated collapsed, Thompson read a message from President Andrew Jackson. In it, the Great White Father told his Indian children that they must migrate. The Indians asked and were given thirty days to consider the President's message. They reconvened on April 22. The next day sixteen Chiefs signed a document agreeing that they and their followers would go west. When five Chiefs either refused to sign or were not present, Thompson, without a vestige of legality, struck their names from the list of leaders. Osceola, when called upon to sign, drew out his knife and plunged it through the document. "This is my mark, and I will make no other," he is said to have cried.*

---

* There is doubt that this incident actually took place at this particular council or, in fact, that it ever occurred at all. The Treaty of Fort Gibson does have a gash, as if made by a knife.

With relations between the Seminole and the Federal Government rapidly deteriorating, there next occurred an incident that would have fateful consequences. According to Thompson's report, dated June 3: "A few days before, Osceola . . . who has thrown more embarrassment in my way than any other, came to my office and insulted me by some insolent remarks. . . . I confined him in irons." Osceola is said to "have raged like a wild animal." Thompson, of course, knew that "to chain an Indian was to degrade him to the utmost." The next day Osceola was able to secure his freedom by signing a document agreeing to migrate. However, the red man's opposition to western migration was not lessened one whit, and he never forgave Thompson, who would soon pay dearly for Osceola's signature.

During the summer and early fall, relations between the whites and Indians did not improve. In mid-June seven white men caught five Seminole hunting outside their reservation. They overpowered the Indians and gave them a flogging. When several other Indians came to the rescue and opened fire, an Indian was fatally shot and three of the whites were wounded. In August, a mail courier, Private Kinsley H. Dalton, was killed. In October, an Indian Chief, Charles Emathla, who had agreed to go west, was shot and killed by Osceola. Meanwhile, as has been stated, communication between Fort Brooke and Fort King became completely disrupted.

On December 26, at about the time Major Dade and his command were approaching the Withlacoochee River, Osceola and a group of about forty of his followers arrived in the vicinity of Fort King. Carefully concealing themselves in a hammock about 600 yards from the main gate, they had a good view not only of the post but also of the buildings outside the palisade, including the Indian agency office and the log house of the post sutler, Erastos Robers. There they awaited their opportunity.

The Indians were concealed there when Lieutenant Colonel Fanning, pursuant to orders he had received from the North, left the fort with three of his four companies for Fort Drane, twenty miles northwest, where General Clinch was concentrating his forces.

At mid-afternoon on December 28, Osceola's chance came. General Thompson and Lieutenant Constantine Smith, having finished their supper, decided on a stroll outside the palisade. They passed the agency office and were about 200 yards from the sutler's store when a shot rang out. It was from Osceola's rifle, given him by his friend Wiley Thompson, that the shot was fired. A ragged volley of shooting followed. Thompson was hit by fourteen balls. Lieutenant Smith was also killed. With savage screeches, the warriors next encircled the sutler's house, where they found and killed the trader and four of his employees, including a boy. Having waited only long enough to take scalps (including those of Thompson and Smith), the red men, following their leader Osceola, withdrew to the palmettos and high grass surrounding the fort. The surprise had been complete and the affair had ended before even one soldier emerged from the stockade gate. Not a shot had been fired in defense of the murdered men.

Thereafter, Osceola and his followers traveled south, and that night they joined other Seminole warriors who were jubilantly celebrating the defeat of Brevet Major Dade's command. Micanopy and Abraham had not waited for their War Chief after all.

Earlier that same day, December 28, 1835, the detachment of 108 men led by Brevet Major Dade had moved out of its bivouac area a few miles north of the Little Withlacoochee River and resumed its northward march along the primitive military road that ran from Fort Brooke on Tampa Bay to Fort King in central Florida.

Massacre of the Whites by th[e]

The above is intended to represent the horrid Massacre of the Whites in F[lorida]
near Four Hundred (including women and childre[n]

Wood Engraving

The cold, steady drizzle made both men and officers uncomfortable. The troopers accordingly wore their sky-blue overcoats buttoned over their ammunition belts. In spite of the chill, hordes of pine flies buzzed about the heads of the marching men.

The principal reason the column had not made better time

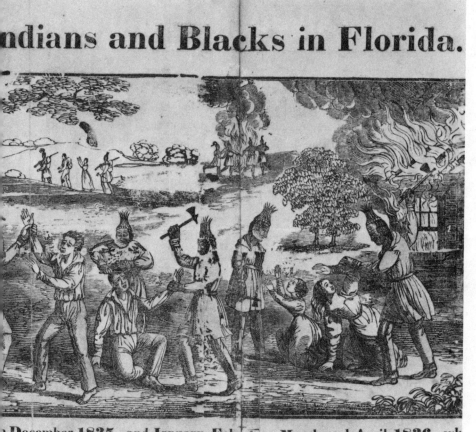

ndians and Blacks in Florida.

December 1835, and January, February, March and April 1836, wh
ctims to the barbarity of the Negroes and Indians.

on its hundred-mile march to Fort King was the deep sand, into which sank the wheels of the wagons and the caisson of the six-pounder. The expedition, in a column of twos, had left Fort Brooke two days before Christmas.

They were now in open "white man's country," their destination but thirty miles away. Major Dade was more relaxed than he had been since assuming the command. Even before leaving Fort Brooke he had been apprehensive, but now he was satisfied that the worst period of danger was past.

Until today he had sent out an advance guard and flankers, but he had concluded that the Indians did not plan to strike. Had they had any such intentions, they had certainly missed several golden opportunities. Back during the crossing of the Hillsborough River the troops had been "sitting ducks." Now that the forks of the Withlacoochee were crossed, Dade felt it was no longer necessary to subject the flankers to the cruel cuts of the palmettos.

Confident, Dade spurred his horse to the head of the column and called out, "You men be of good heart! Our difficulties and dangers are over now. As soon as we arrive at Fort King, you'll have three days' rest and gaily keep Christmas."

Dade had hardly finished speaking when a single shot rang out. Those in the forward ranks gasped in horror as they saw the major slump in his saddle and slowly, almost gracefully, fall to the ground. The column came to a halt.

The major's body had barely touched the earth when, but twenty yards from the troops on the left flank, a horde of wildly yelling Indians and Negroes sprang from the tall grass and palmettos and fired at the halted troops at point-blank range. Fifty soldiers fell. Pandemonium reigned as the savage cries of the attackers mingled with the screams of the wounded.

Half the command's enlisted personnel and four of its officers were casualties. Before the Seminole could reload and let go another volley, Captain George Washington Gardiner assumed command. The men sprang into action. Shedding their heavy coats, they took positions behind the trees on each side of the road. Lieutenant William Bessenger and his crew rushed the six-pounder forward and opened fire, the gunners becoming prime targets for the attackers.

Against an attacking force of 160 warriors the remaining soldiers were badly outnumbered, but once discipline took over they began giving a good account of themselves. Their enemy became less venturesome and the firing more sporadic. The canister shot from the gun dulled any Seminole enthusiasm for a charge on the beleaguered soldiers.

The Indians and their allies broke off action, withdrew into the woods, and the firing ceased. The first attack had ended.

Captain Gardiner took stock of his situation. He found he had about thirty able-bodied men. Of these he put twenty soldiers to work felling trees and building a redoubt. He ordered the remainder to bring in the wounded and salvage ammunition from the dead.

The irregular log breastwork took the shape of a triangle with its apex toward the enemy on the northwest and its base parallel to the road, with the pond at the rear. On the outside of the barricade the captain placed the gun.

The Indians' line of attack had thus been reduced to approximately 100 feet. They soon regrouped to face the redoubt on all three sides.

Before long the battle resumed, the exposed gun crew still the principal target of the enemy. But as one cannoneer fell his place was quickly taken by another soldier from within the breastwork.

The six-pounder continued to spit out its message of death until all the ammunition was exhausted. The Indians were then able to concentrate their attack on the men within the enclave.

Methodically the warriors picked off their prey. Captain Gardiner took four bullets. As his life ebbed away, he called out, "I can give you no more orders; do your best." The surgeon, John Gatlin, fell on the two double-barreled shotguns he had been firing. Lieutenant Richard Henderson took a bullet in his forehead. Finally Lieutenant Bessenger was the last soldier standing in the barricade. A ball passed through both his thighs and he collapsed. The firing ceased.

Cautiously the Seminole, led by Chiefs Micanopy, Jumper, and Alligator, approached the redoubt. They searched the bodies, stripped them of insignia and gathered up the weapons. They took no scalps, nor did they subject their fallen enemy to any other indignity. They removed the six-pounder from its carriage and threw it into the pond.

As they finished their gruesome task, a blood-smeared figure, musician Joseph Wilson, sprang up. In a single blow he brained one of the warriors, leapt over the barricade and fled. He was shot down by two mounted red men.

The Indians withdrew to the west. Their place was rapidly taken by some fifty Negro allies of the Seminole. With axes and knives they made short shrift of any white man who showed signs of life. Quickly they stripped the bodies of shoes and coats and hurried away. The silence of death prevailed.

In spite of the Seminole and Negro precautions, not all of the white men were dead. Private Ransome Clarke of B Company, Second Regiment, was the first to regain consciousness. Merciful darkness hid the horror of the enclosure from him.

With a broken arm and a bullet through one lung, he began crawling about the stockade. Groping, he touched another soldier whose chest still moved. Private Edwin De Courcy, though wounded, had also been missed by the Negro butchery.

Clutching each other for support, the two men painfully dragged themselves from the redoubt. Almost without hope they turned south and started for Fort Brooke, sixty miles away. Miraculously, Private Clarke would survive his incredible journey to Fort Brooke, where he would report the massacre.

Only one other soldier, a Private Joseph, survived the battle. In the first annihilating volley, his arm was shattered. Throwing himself into the nearby pond, he kept his nose above water until he was sure the enemy was gone. When

darkness came he left the pond's protection and started for Fort
Brooke.

And so ended what was to become known as Dade's Massacre.[10] It was to be the first battle of a long and cruel war,
which would end, after seven years of fighting, as a Pyrrhic
victory for the Indians and their Negro allies. The price would
be the nearly complete destruction of the Seminole Nation.

How and why did this conflict between the Indians and Negroes on one side and the whites on the other develop into a
major war? We must look to the history of the combatants, of
the people and the land, to understand fully the forces that led
to Dade's Massacre, the murder of Indian agent Thompson, and
a seven-year war that destroyed an American nation.

CHAPTER II

The Indian
Seminole

. . . painted, fearless, uncontrolled, and free.

WILLIAM BARTRAM, 1774

The Indians who in the sixteenth century greeted the early Spanish explorers in Florida were probably of Mayan descent, their ancestors having emigrated from Yucatan as early as 8500 B.C. Some of them, the Apalachees, for example, can be traced to the headwaters of the Guaviare stem of the Orinoco River in South America.[1] Numbering as many as 25,000, they were roughly divided into three tribes. The Apalachees lived in western Florida as far east as the Aucilla River. Various tribes of Timucua-speaking Indians inhabited the rest of northern Florida as far south as a line running roughly from Tampa Bay to Cape Canaveral. The Calusa occupied southern Florida. By the mid-1800s, all of these aborigines were virtually extinct, the victims primarily of the struggle for empire of the European colonizing powers.

The peaceful, friendly Apalachees were the first to suffer at

20

the hands of the whites. In 1704 Colonial Governor James
Moore of South Carolina, with a small contingent of militia and
a thousand Lower Creek Indians, invaded western Florida,
destroying Spanish missions and Indian towns as he went. He
took as prisoners 300 Indian men and 1,000 women and children,
many of whom were sold into slavery in the West Indies. Slave
raids from the English-speaking colonies; wars with the Spanish;
and diseases brought by the white man, including measles,
chicken pox, mumps, and that forerunner of Western civilization,
syphilis, to which the Indians had no immunity; all tended to
reduce the ranks of the Timucuans. In 1705 alone, thirty-two
Indian villages in northern Florida were destroyed by slave-
hungry English raiders. Creek raids instigated by the English,
and emigration to Key West and Cuba to avoid such forays,
ended the Calusa Indians' reign along the lower Gulf Coast,
where they were said to have numbered 15,000 in 1566. In
1764, when the Spanish relinquished St. Augustine to the English, they took with them some eighty-nine Yamasees, practically
the last of the aborigines.

Mahon notes that a population vacuum had been created:

> A habitable vacuum, recently peopled, now devoid of popula-
> tion except for a thin fringe of white men principally along the
> east coast. Into this inviting void there moved from time to time
> during a century, groups of Indians from the territories north
> of the peninsula. Nearly all of them were of the Muskogean fam-
> ily and were affiliated with the Creek Confederation.[2]

The Creek Confederation was separated into two main divi-
sions. The Upper Creek lived along the Coosa and Tallapoosa
branches of the Alabama River, while the Lower Creek occupied
the valleys of the Chattahoochee and Flint Rivers. The confederation included some sixty towns, almost all located on rivers

throughout Georgia and Alabama. Having different cultures, languages, and environments, and loosely bound together, they rarely had a common goal. The confederation somewhat resembled the Greek city-states in organization. The men of the villages conducted their own affairs and elected their own chief or *mico*, and although he wielded considerable power, this was seldom exercised without consulting the council of principal men. The head man was generally chosen from a specified family, as long as that clan produced qualified leaders. In spite of this hereditary feature, the Creek towns represented probably as pure a democracy as it is possible to achieve.

A man was a member of his mother's family. The hereditary chiefs were picked from a line that descended from the woman. In spite of this, however, the women did most of the drudgery, while the men, when not on the warpath, hunted and fished. Personal property of a household nature belonged to the women. After a divorce, which was easy to obtain, the wife kept the children and her household property.

The Creek were a warlike people, and their mode of distinction was prowess in battle. A man retained his given name and was forced to do menial labor until he had earned a title through valor.

The Creek, besides hunting and fishing, cultivated corn, melons, beans, and pumpkins. They also raised cattle, and those Indians with large herds were accorded great respect.

The original tribes of Florida were virtually extinct when the Lower Creek began probing the population vacuum and making permanent settlements on the peninsula. In 1713, following Queen Anne's War, a few bands of Lower Creek made their way from Georgia into northern Florida at the invitation of the Spanish, who wanted a buffer between themselves and the English. From 1739 to 1748, during the War of Jenkins' Ear, bands of Lower Creek ranged over northern Florida as allies of the English. A number remained to found permanent towns.* One such group was the Onconee, who settled in the Alachua area, where they built the town of Cuscowilla. Led by Chief Cowcatcher, founder of the Seminole Nation,[3] they were implacable foes of the Spanish. At about the same time that the Onconees were establishing their settlements, the militant Chiahas were migrating into West Florida. Later, a group of Eufaula left their Chattahoochee River homes and settled north of Tampa Bay.

The word *seminole,* used by the Creek to describe the Florida Indians, literally means "the people whom the Sun God does not love" (i.e., accursed, renegades). They were people who had left their old ways, their land, and their kin, and had gone to a far country. They were accordingly despised by their Creek relatives.

The last and perhaps the most important of the Creek migrations into Florida, for it doubled the Indian population, was that following the defeat of the Red Stick[5] by General Andrew Jackson and his Tennessee Militia in the Creek War, at the battle of Horseshoe Bend, on March 27, 1814. The loss of 800 warriors in that battle forced the Creek Confederacy to submit to the onerous terms that Jackson laid down. The Creek were forced to cede two-thirds of their territory, and many Red Stick, refusing to reconcile themselves to the harsh treaty, fled southward. Among these refugees was a boy whom the whites later called Osceola, or Powell.

---

* According to Doctor Mahon, all the Creek who had migrated to Florida prior to 1767 spoke variations of Hitchiti. The second major tongue, the Muskogee, was introduced by the Eufala in 1767.[4] Most of the Muskogee-speaking Upper Creek were later to settle in the vicinity of Tampa Bay, but a group of Tallahassee built towns in West Florida. Following the outbreak of the American Revolution, a number of pro-English Creek sought comparative safety in British Florida.

The new Florida Indian emigrants, who numbered about 5,000 persons, residing in some twenty-five villages, brought with them most of the habits, customs, and rites they had known in the North. Of necessity, however, some aspects of their culture were modified in accordance with the environment of their new home. William Bartram described a Seminole village in North Central Florida that he visited in 1774:

> . . about thirty habitations, each of which consisted of two houses nearly the same size, about thirty feet in length, twelve feet wide and about the same height. . . . . The houses are constructed of a kind of frame . . .

Each house, he went on, is:

> . . . near the middle of a Square Yard . . . which is always kept carefully swept. Their towns are clean, the inhabitants being particular in laying their filth at a proper distance from their dwelling, which undoubtedly contributes to the healthiness of their inhabitants.[6]

Among the various titles of rank of the Seminole, the highest was that of Mico, a term which many of the white traders translated as "King." Almost always chosen from the same family as his predecessor, he held office for life and was generally succeeded by his nephew in the female line. The name of his town was prefixed to his title. He received all visitors and directed all public and domestic concerns. The Hinijas was next in rank and second in command. He supervised all public works and the cultivation of the fields. He was also in charge of certain of the Indian ceremonials, including the "black drink." The Amathia, or leaders of bands, were given their title as the result of valor in battle. They were the disciplinarians. Whites generally called them Chiefs. Warriors of recognized bravery were called Tustenuggee. Others were called Hadjo, or those of frenzied valor.

Their sexual code, although more liberal than that of the whites, was much more rigidly adhered to. Intercourse before marriage was permitted. If a child resulted, the mother could destroy it, but more often the infant was adopted by her relatives. Not only was adultery forbidden, but both partners were subject to severe punishments, including the cropping of nose and ears. Men, if they could afford them, were permitted several wives.

The disciplining of children was left entirely to the mothers, or to their brothers, never to the fathers. The punishment, which was certainly not that of a permissive society, included the scratching of a child's skin until blood flowed, so that the evil might be let out.

The formation of a war party was often an individual decision. If a warrior could not get the support of the chief and his council he was permitted to recruit followers for his proposed expedition. However, the leader of such a group might pay with his life if the attack was unsuccessful.

Once a war had been agreed upon, no draft mechanism was necessary. As a man's standing was determined by his conduct in battle, there were no recruiting problems or any desertions.

Ownership of slaves carried status, and so there were occasional slave-stealing raids into Georgia and Alabama. The pleasant, almost free, life of their slaves also made the Seminole Nation a mecca for runaways from the North. Having once been taken under the protection of an Indian warrior, the fugitive could rest assured that any whites following him with guns and dogs would be given short shrift by his new friends.

By the Treaty of Paris in 1783 Florida reverted to Spain, but the Spanish were too weak to really govern their returned province. The Creek émigrés, or Seminole as they were now called, accordingly had complete control over a vast area, in which, as Mahon writes:

> . . . there were deer in abundance, even bison awhile, to say nothing of the herds of cattle running from abandoned Spanish ranches. In addition to the ample and varied supplies of meats, there were a wide variety of vegetables, berries and fruits.[7]

And William Bartram reported that Florida:

> . . . furnishes such a plenty and variety of supplies for the nourishment and variety of animals, that I can venture to assert that no part of the globe so abounds with wild game and creatures fit for the food of man. . . . Thus [the Seminole are] contented and undisturbed [and] they appear as blithe and free as the birds of the air, and like them volatile and active, tuneful and vociferous. The visage, action, and deportment of the Seminole, form the most striking picture of happiness in this life.[8]

The Seminole, almost without opposition, had taken over a bountiful country. In it, they were leading the affluent life. Their nominal overlords, the Spanish, could barely hold a handful of towns along the coast. Florida had become these Indians' new home, and a happy one. It was not likely that they would ever voluntarily relinquish this new-found land.

CHAPTER III

The Negro
Seminole

This [the Seminole conflict] . . . is
a Negro, not an Indian, War.

MAJOR GENERAL
THOMAS SIDNEY JESUP, 1836

In the year 1687, in an open boat, there arrived in St. Augustine eighteen Negroes, eight men and ten women, who had fled slavery in the English settlement of St. George. They were kindly received and given asylum by the Spanish authorities. While they might not have been the first to seek freedom in Florida, their arrival and reception certainly indicates that at an early date that Territory became a haven for fugitive blacks from the North.

While slavery existed under Spanish rule, it was considerably different from that practiced in the English colonies. Not only were the Spanish slave codes considerably more lenient than those to the North, but Negroes were given more freedom. As Robert L. Anderson notes: ". . . there is no record of a Negro slave fleeing from the Spanish to the English."[1]

By 1736 the arrival of fugitive slaves from the North singly

27

or in groups was no longer a novelty, and their numbers were showing a steady yearly increase. In 1739 the Spanish Governor of Florida reported in a letter to his king from St. Augustine that he had "put at liberty various fugitive slaves" and sent them "to live in the Territory . . . half a league more or less to the North. . . ."² Later a military post, Fort Moosa, or Old Fort, was established nearby for the protection of these former slaves.

As early as 1750, a number of the escaping slaves were no longer seeking asylum from the Spanish authorities, but rather were asking the Seminole for protection. They were welcomed by the Indians.

The Seminole held slaves, both Indian and Negro, but the institution was unlike that under both the English and the Spanish. More vassal than slave, the Negro, or on occasion a captured Indian, was permitted considerable freedom. The slaves lived by themselves, generally in a village, and there was little or no supervision of their activities. Colonel Gad Humphreys, the Indian agent, wrote, "The Negroes of the Seminole Indians are wholly independent . . . and are slaves but in name; they work only when it suits their inclination." True, they were required to give to their masters a small percentage of their harvest and of the domestic animals they slaughtered, but the amount taken was "generally less than an Englishman or a Spaniard would pay in taxes." In return, they received protection from the whites, particularly from the slave catchers. They were expected to give military service to the Indians, but actually such service was almost on a voluntary basis. They seldom lost an opportunity to fight their enemy, the whites, and were often said to be more cunning and fierce warriors than the Indians. A red man might on occasion show mercy to a fallen foe, but a Negro, remembering his past treatment at the hands of the whites, permitted himself no such leniency. In 1812 Colonel Daniel Newnan of the Georgia Militia spoke of Seminole Negroes as ". . . their [the Indians'] best soldiers."

The Negro slaves of the Seminole were permitted to marry and raise families. On rare occasion, they married Indians and were immediately given their freedom and went to live in a Seminole village.

Dr. Kenneth Wiggins Porter, professor of history of the University of Oregon, wrote in the *Journal of Southern History:*

> A system of relationship between the Seminole Indians and their Negroes developed which was the admiration or horror of all beholders. The Negroes lived in separate villages of well-built houses, raised crops of corn, sweet potatoes, other vegetables and even cotton, and possessed herds of livestock; their masters, or rather protectors, never presumed to meddle with any of this property so long as they received a reasonable "tribute." . . . The Negroes also had plenty of time for hunting and fishing, and under this almost idyllic regime they throve amazingly. Dressed in the easy Indian costume they were, according to one observer, stout and even gigantic in their persons . . . the finest looking people I have ever seen.[3]

The slaves of the Seminole were of four groups: those that had been born among the Indians and knew only that life, those that had been captured on raids across the Georgia or Alabama border, those that had come to the Seminole as fugitives, and those who on occasion were purchased from the whites. The latter three groups made by far the better warriors.

The Negroes had a good ear for languages, and many of the Seminole Negroes not only spoke the English and Spanish of the whites, but quickly learned the Muskogee and Hitchiti of their protectors. A few even knew how to read and write. A number of the more intelligent of the Negroes rose to positions of great authority in the Seminole Nation. As many of these black leaders became well known, whites charged that they actually governed the Seminole. Governor William DuVal stated in 1826 that "the Indian-Negroes were a bad influence on their Seminole masters," and most white Floridians of the time agreed with him.

Perhaps the best known of the Negroes who rose to power in the Seminole Nation was Abraham, Prime Minister, Sensebearer, and Chancellor for Micanopy, of the Cowkeeper Dynasty, a principal Chief of the Seminole and head of the Acachua. This Indian leader was said never to have made a decision without consulting his Negro advisor.

One of the remarkable personalities of American history, Abraham was of middle age when, prior to the Seminole War, he became a figure of national importance.

Abraham is generally believed to have been born between 1787 and 1798, probably in Georgia or one of the other English-speaking states—for although he had lived in Pensacola, there is no evidence that he had any knowledge of Spanish. General McCall, who probably knew him longer and more intimately than any other white man, recorded that as a youth, Abraham was a slave, the domestic servant of a physician, Doctor Sierra of Pensacola.

In July of 1814, during the War of 1812, over a hundred men in two sloops, under the command of Major Edward Nicholls, a British Marine, occupied Pensacola. To swell his small force, the major enlisted and armed a number of Red Stick Creek Indians and as many slaves as a promise of freedom and land in the British West Indies would bring to his colors. Among the recruits soon drilling was the Negro youth Abraham. Early in November, General Andrew Jackson stormed Pensacola, and General Nicholls, his British troops, and his Indian and Negro allies, including Abraham, were forced to evacuate that city. Having sailed to the Apalachicola River, Nicholls built a fort at a spot called Prospect Bluff, some fifteen miles

Abraham, about 1835

from the river's mouth. There he remained until June 1815. Before leaving, he turned over the fort, with its supplies, quantities of ammunition, and ten heavy guns, to his Red Stick and Negro allies.

Setting sail for London, he took with him a half-breed Upper Creek Chief, Joseph Francis, on whom Tecumseh had conferred the title of Prophet. Thereafter the fort, now called Fort Negro, gradually became a haven for slaves escaping from the United States. Affording protection to hundreds of runaways, it was to become such a burr under the saddle of the American slaveholders that in July 1816 a naval and land force, under the overall command of Lieutenant Colonel Duncan L. Clinch, was dispatched south by the American government to invade Spanish territory and destroy Fort Negro. On July 24 one of the blockading gunboats scored a lucky hit on the fort's magazine, killing 270 of the defenders and wounding all the others. A number of the Indians and blacks who were not in the fort at the time escaped to distant Seminole villages.

Abraham was one of the survivors. After the explosion, he made his way to a Suwannee River town. There, at the time of the Battle of Suwannee, during the 1818 invasion of Florida, he fought with the Indians against the troops of General Andrew Jackson. In the battle he is said to have won his war title, "Sauanaffe Tustunnugee," which can be roughly translated as Suwannee Warrior. At a later date, Abraham put himself under the protection of Micanopy, principal Chief of the Alachua, and thereafter lived in the Negro town of Pilaklinkaha, or Many Ponds.

In 1826 Micanopy headed a delegation of Seminole Chiefs who visited Washington at the invitation of the government. He selected Abraham as interpreter for the group. The Negro apparently made quite an impression on the Chiefs, for on his return he was rewarded with the gift of a young wife, Hagar, the widow of Chief Bowlegs. She was to bear Abraham several

Group of Seminole Chiefs who visited Washington in 1826. Micanopy is seated third from left; behind him is Abraham.

sons and a daughter. Abraham was also the principal interpreter at Paynes' Landing in May 1832, and he accompanied the delegation of Chiefs that went west to Fort Gibson Indian Territory in 1833 to inspect the land to which the government was planning to move the Seminole.

Abraham later played a leading role in the decision for war, and the importance of his leadership was recognized both by army officers and Territorial officials.

When war finally came in late 1835, Abraham openly participated in the conflict, leading a command of about a hundred Negro and Indian warriors. No action, the Indians said, was complete "unless Abraham was in it." Leading his company, he participated in the ambush and annihilation of Major Dade's command, in the first and second battles of the Withlacoochee and at the Battle of Big Cypress Swamp.

33

Following the abortive treaty of March 6, 1837, Abraham remained in Major General Thomas S. Jesup's hands. He was shipped west from Tampa with his family on February 25, 1839.

In the period just prior to the start of the war, John Caesar, a Seminole Negro who was closely associated with Abraham, played a leading role in the Florida story. He was a Negro who had been raised among the Seminole. His parents had been fugitive slaves, so besides Muskogee, he spoke English fluently. He was to occupy the stage for only a little over a year, but he was to exercise a profound influence on the course of the War.

John Caesar was a slave or vassal of Emathca (called King Philip by the whites), a brother-in-law of Micanopy and the principal Chief of the Indians along the St. Johns River. He occupied roughly the same relationship to his master as Abraham did to Micanopy—interpreter, counselor, and Chief of the Negro retainers. He was admitted even by the whites to be extremely intelligent, "an aggressive, smart Negro."

A man in his early sixties at the outbreak of the Seminole War, he was short and stocky and had a rather broad face. He did not have the charisma of Abraham, but he was acknowledged to be next to him among the Negroes in importance in the Seminole Nation. Caesar was said to have a Negro wife on one of the plantations and prior to the War was often seen visiting among the slaves. It was apparently easy for him and Abraham, up until Dade's Massacre, to visit the St. Johns River plantations for the purpose of persuading slaves to join with the Seminole once the War started. They were successful beyond their wildest hopes, for upward of two hundred and fifty Negroes joined the Seminole at the start of hostilities. Before taking off, many of the revolting slaves plundered and burned the plantations. Brigadier General Joseph M. Hernandez, who commanded the militia in the St. Augustine area, said, "This is the very worst feature of the whole of this war."

King Philip, Second Chief, by George Catlin, 1837

Almost a year later, John Caesar was again heard from in a military role. He evidently had determined on his own to inaugurate a guerrilla campaign in the St. Augustine area. Planning several units, he first gathered about himself a group of thirteen men: eight fugitive slaves, two Indian Negroes, a freed Negro, and two Indians.

Contact was made with slaves in St. Augustine, who furnished the guerrillas with supplies as well as ammunition. For such a force, horses were needed, and on January 17, 1837, a raid was made on the plantation of John M. Hanson, only two miles from St. Augustine. Unfortunately for the guerrillas, an alarm was raised and they were driven off. A Captain Hans took up the trail with a large force, followed them for a day and came upon their camp on the Williams farm, around thirty miles from St. Augustine, at about ten o'clock at night. Satisfied that they had avoided pursuit, the raiders were carelessly lounging around their fire. The white troops were able to get close to the camp without being detected. Firing a volley at almost point-blank range, they killed three of the guerrillas and seriously wounded a fourth. The rest of the raiders took off in confusion. Those killed included Joe Merritt and John Caesar.

The campaign of John Caesar had been a tactical failure, but nevertheless it was to have a profound influence on the course of the War. Not only were troops vitally needed elsewhere tied down to protecting St. Augustine and the other towns, but the fear of God had been put into the whites.

Among the supplies found in Caesar's camp were many articles that had been purchased within the week in St. Augustine. The loyal Negroes had not proven very loyal. The possibility of a general slave insurrection, always a nagging fear in the subconscious minds of the slaveholders, came into the open. Such a rebellion, in combination with the conflict being fought with the Seminole, could well result in a war that could not be won by the white man. There was also the danger that the rebellion

36

would spread to the North. This nightmare haunted the sleep of Major General Thomas S. Jesup, Army Commander in Florida at the time of John Caesar's death.

Loyalty to their Negro allies was a characteristic of the Seminole both before and during the War. There can be little doubt that, had the Indians been willing to refuse asylum and turn over the Negro fugitives to the Territorial government, there would have been no war. On a number of occasions during the conflict peace terms certainly could have been agreed upon, had the Indians been willing to sacrifice their Negro friends.

By 1820 it was recognized throughout the slave-holding states that a Seminole enclave in Florida was a threat to slavery. The conflict that followed was the only Indian war that the United States fought not for land but rather to defend the institution of slavery.

Historian Kenneth Porter wrote:

> Sentiment for the removal of the Seminole Negroes preceded that for Indian removal. As early as 1821 the Florida Indian agent said of "the marone [i.e., maroon] Negroes, who live among the Indians" that it would "be necessary to remove from the Floridians this group of lawless freebooters, among whom runaway Negroes will always find a refuge," although he admitted that if force were employed the Indians would always take the Negroes' part. It was soon recognized that it was impossible to persuade the Indians to rid Florida of a "serious nuisance" by selling their Negroes, because of the Indians' serious attachment to them. The bodily removal of the Indians themselves was increasingly regarded as the only solution of the Negro problem.[4]

CHAPTER IV

The Americans

We hold these Truths to be self-evident;
that all Men are created equal; that they
are endowed by their Creator with certain
unalienable Rights; that among these are
Life, Liberty and the pursuit of Happiness . . .

THOMAS JEFFERSON, 1776

The Treaty of Paris not only recognized the independence of the United States but also returned Florida to Spain. The fledgling nation to the north was to continue, however, to be the implacable enemy of the Seminole.

The thirteen colonies had been settled not by adventurers, but by true colonists, men who wanted land, the one commodity that in the old country carried with it stability and security. Consequently, the Americans, first as colonists and then as citizens of the new republic, were never able peacefully to coexist with the Indians. Always they coveted the land on which the neighboring "savages" lived. So long as they remained colonists, the Crown exercised some restraining influence, but once they were on their own, there was no one to hold their greed in check. In the Southeast they not only wanted the land the Indians still held, but felt that Florida by all the laws of nature should be a part of the United States. There followed frequent raids into Spanish territory, which the government of the United States did nothing to suppress.

The years between 1763 and 1783, during which Florida was an English territory, were happy and prosperous years for the Seminole. The British rod was lightly used, and the Seminole felt a security they had seldom known. Accordingly, during the American Revolution they were pro-British and intensified their cattle- and slave-stealing raids across the border.

Following the Revolution, William Augustus Bowles, an American Tory from Maryland who had seen his family persecuted for their pro-British views, came among the Seminole. He first arrived in Florida at the age of fifteen as an ensign in a loyalist regiment sent to defend Pensacola. Thereafter he went to live with the Indians, learned their language and customs, and married the daughter of Chief Prettyman. Later he attempted to found a new nation, with himself as its head. Calling himself Director-General of the State of Muskogee, he was able to draw around him a number of Seminole bands. In establishing lines of communication with the British he had only a little early success. He died in a Spanish prison, with his dream unfulfilled. All that he achieved was a worsening of relations between the Seminole and the Americans to the North.

Although the Seminole were still pro-British at the start of the War of 1812, they were disinclined to participate in actual conflict. The Georgians, however, determined that Florida should become a territory of the United States, were responsible for a number of border incidents that rankled the Indians. It didn't take much persuasion on the part of Kindelan, the anti-American Spanish Governor of Florida, to convince the Seminole that they should retaliate through a series of harassing actions along the Georgian border. The Georgians were quick to

Nea-Math-La, 1836 lithograph

reply. In late September 1812, determined to destroy Indian power once and for all, Colonel Daniel Newnan led a force of Georgia Militia a hundred miles south of the border. The expedition was a near disaster. Attacked by the Seminole and their ferocious Negro allies in a running engagement lasting almost two weeks, Newnan was barely able to escape to the North with a portion of his command intact.

In February 1813 the Americans struck again, this time, however, with a regiment of 250 mounted Tennessee Volunteers and a detachment of Regulars. In a campaign that lasted but three weeks the white troops are said to have destroyed 386 Indian houses and 2000 bushels of corn, as well as herds of horses and cattle. The Seminole of northern Florida were badly defeated, and it was some time before they recovered.

Meanwhile in Alabama, within the Creek Nation, a civil war erupted between the Upper and Lower Creek. The fighting soon led to white intervention, with a standard three-prong invasion of the Upper Creek country. On March 27, 1814, General Andrew Jackson, commanding Tennessee Militia, decisively defeated the Red Stick at Horseshoe Bend. The power of the Creek Nation was broken, and the Seminole lost a buffer on their left flank that had protected them from the whites.

Anger at the destruction of Fort Negro in 1816 next brought the Mikasukis, a branch of the Seminole, to the center of the stage. In November 1817 Neamathla, the Chief of their village of Fowltown, sent a message to Major General Edmund P. Gaines at nearby Fort Scott. If the Americans dared cross the Flint River to cut wood, they would be destroyed. Neamathla was probably supported in his action by Chief Bowlegs of the Alachua.[1] Fowltown was within American territory, and General Gaines, indignant at what he considered an impertinence, dispatched Major David E. Twiggs, a Georgian, with a force of 250 men, to arrest Neamathla. An indecisive small-arms action ensued which has been called the opening engagement of the *First* Seminole War.*

Later the Indians in the same area attacked a force of forty men under the command of Lieutenant Richard W. Scott of the Seventh Infantry. Scott, a Virginian who had entered the army as an ensign in 1813, was coming up the Apalachicola River to Fort Scott. Thirty-four of the whites, including seven soldiers' wives, were killed.

Gaines now joined General Jackson in urging that a punitive expedition be sent into Florida to chastise the Seminole. "Jamie" Monroe in Washington was his usual indecisive self. Gaines was first advised that such action was not advisable. A week later, after news of the Scott disaster had reached Washington, Gaines was told that he could send out his troops at his own discretion. Next, he was advised that he could cross the border but was not to attack the Seminole near a Spanish fort. Finally, directly after Christmas, the War Department ordered General Andrew Jackson to take command, and "bring the Seminole under control." Before Jackson received his orders, Gaines advanced on Fowltown on January 4, 1818, found it deserted, and burned it to the ground.

Jackson arrived at Fort Scott in early March, and he was soon headed south with 500 Regulars, 1,000 Tennessee Militia, and 2,000 Creek warrior allies. The Seminole, short of ammunition, offered little resistance to the whites. The only opposition came from a group of several hundred Negro warriors, who, upon the Seminole withdrawal, fought as a delaying rear guard.

---

* The author here follows the historian's convention of separating the Seminole conflict into three distinct Seminole Wars: the series of small engagements from 1817 to 1818, the major period of struggle from 1835 to 1842, and a third outbreak of fighting from 1855 to 1858. Since the middle period marked the most intense and decisive action between the Seminole and the U.S. government, that is the primary subject of this book, although it also covers, as here, the earlier and later fighting. —Editor

Armed only with outmoded muskets and outnumbered by at least six to one, they were still able to delay Jackson's army until all of the Indian towns in the zone of the advance could be evacuated.

By late April, Jackson, having completed the destruction of the villages west of the Suwannee, set about what he considered the real purpose of the expedition—the conquest of Florida. There is little doubt that he was confident that he had at least the tacit approval of the Monroe Administration for his subsequent actions. By May 28 he had taken both St. Marks and Pensacola.

Just prior to Jackson's capture of St. Marks, an American naval ship with supplies for the American Army entered the port. To avoid the possibility of being fired upon by the Spanish, it flew English colors. Thinking the ship was British, the Prophet Francis, who had recently returned from London, and an old Red Stick Chief, Homollimicke, allowed themselves to be enticed aboard. The two Indians were seized and, on Jackson's orders, promptly hanged.

During the course of the campaign Jackson took prisoner two traders, Alexander Arbuthnot and Robert Ambrister, who made Cedar Keys their base. Both men were British subjects. Convicted by a drumhead court-martial of inciting the Indians to hostilities, they also swung from the yardarm.

Having ordered General Gaines to take St. Augustine, Jackson left on May 30 for Tennessee. Reporting to the Secretary of War that Florida was now American, he noted, "I will assure you Cuba will be ours in a few days."

In Tennessee Jackson learned that his expectation of support by the Monroe Administration had been unduly optimistic. Not only was the cabinet split down the middle, but in both the Senate and the House resolutions had been introduced proposing to censure him for his naked aggression. In August 1818 President Monroe decided to return Florida to Spain.

43

Jackson arrived in Washington in January 1819 and found that in spite of Monroe's action the controversy still raged. For a while it seemed likely that a resolution of censure against Jackson might prevail, but his popularity throughout the country was too much for his opponents. The man in the street regarded him as a hero who had humbled both perfidious Albion and papist Spain. As one citizen was heard to remark to another, "I believe you as much as if General Jackson or Jesus Christ had said it." Congress failed to take any action, and Jackson seems to have remained in the good graces of President Monroe.

Spain, however, had seen the handwriting on the wall—by attempting to hold Florida, she might lose it without any compensation. Accordingly, she offered the territory to the United States for a consideration of $18,000,000. (It would later be bought for $5,000,000.) On Washington's birthday, February 22, 1821, ratifications of a treaty of cession were exchanged. A clause of the treaty read:

> The inhabitants of the territories which his Catholic Majesty cedes to the United States shall be incorporated in the Union of the United States, as soon as may be consistent with the principles of the Federal Constitution, and admitted to the enjoyment of all the privileges, rights, and immunities of the citizens of the United States.

The United States had thus pledged itself to the speedy granting of citizenship to both the Seminole and the free Negroes of Florida. Certainly at the time of signing or of ratification the Americans had no intention of making the Florida Indians citizens, let alone the Negroes. His Catholic Majesty had, however, insisted on such a clause to soothe his conscience. The Americans for their part were determined to get Florida and, once it was in their possession, to do with it as they pleased. That of course was exactly what was done. The treaty was regarded as but a scrap of paper.

As it entered the sixth decade of its existence, the United States had more problems than those posed by the Seminole. The nation continued to be prosperous, but in the White House, Andrew Jackson, a bitter and enfeebled old man, with fifteen months of his presidency remaining, was laying the foundation for the depression that would plague his successor.

The Second United States Bank had collapsed, but throughout the country local bankers expanded credit, building a structure that would soon come crashing down on their heads. The Administration boasted that for the first time in the nation's history, it had paid off the public debt—but in doing so it had abandoned internal improvement. The large network of roads and canals made necessary by economic growth had accordingly been financed by state and municipal governments. The Federal debt had been paid, but at the local level. Over a period of twenty years public obligations had increased fifteenfold. Congress was not concerned. Its principal worry seemed to be how to spend the surplus that was flowing into the central Treasury. Deflation would ultimately solve the problem for the Congress.

The question of slavery was considered resolved by the Missouri Compromise of 1820, but the possibility of annexing the newly formed Republic of Texas again brought it to the fore. Not only those in the growing abolitionist movement but also a considerable body of citizens with less extreme views were bitterly opposed to any extension of the nation's borders in the slave-holding South.

There were also international clouds on the horizon. The French had not paid the spoliation claims as promised, and Andy Jackson had threatened them with the use of force. Jackson did not explain how so small a nation, even a young and vigorous one, with a population of only 12,866,020 citizens, could by itself bring mighty France to her knees.

The Army of the United States, although yearly growing more professional, was still minuscule in 1835, compared to those of the European powers. The Secretary of War was Lewis Cass, who had publicly announced his belief that the American Navy was the first line of defense. A veteran of the War of 1812 and a major general in the Ohio Militia, Cass, who had personally witnessed one of the nation's most humiliating disasters, the surrender of Detroit by General William Hull in 1812, had no real confidence in the army. Before coming to Washington, the Secretary had served ably for eighteen years as Governor of the Territory of Michigan. In 1835, however, he was tired and ill, and he retained few of the illusions of his youth.

Next in the army chain of command was Alexander Macomb, the Commanding General—an office created in 1821, vaguely similar to the present Chief of Staff. Appointed to his post in 1828, Macomb was not a strong man, and during his tenure the office became almost honorary. More often than not the President and the Secretary of War dealt with the field commanders through the Adjutant General.

Under Macomb were three brigadier generals, Winfield Scott, Edmund Pendleton Gaines, and Thomas S. Jesup. Scott, the ablest of the three, was a bitter rival of Gaines. The two men hated each other. Jesup was the Quartermaster General. In addition to the three brigadier generals, there were the Adjutant General, the Inspector General, the Commissary General of Substance, the Commissary General of Purchase, the Chief of Engineers, the Chief of Ordnance, the Surgeon General and the Paymaster General, all of whom were colonels.

While none of the general officers was a graduate of the United States Military Academy, the bulk of the field- and company-grade officers, of whom there were almost 600, were from West Point. The school on the Hudson had, however, become quite unpopular throughout the country, and both Jackson and his party favored its abolition. The opponents of the Academy insisted that the cadets were "only taught to fight European style, making them useless in their principal role of opposing the Redmen." Furthermore, an aristocratic tradition was being bred in the school's graduates. West Point, with the prestige of having been founded by Jefferson, managed to survive each of the onslaughts.

There was a shade of truth in the charge that the Academy was creating a military aristocracy, for most of its graduates did come from the "better" families, and many of the sons of officers were following in their fathers' footsteps. However, these young men were certainly not seeking a military career for financial return. A major general, of whom there was but one, received only $4,590 a year; a brigadier, $3,000; a colonel, $1,776; a lieutenant colonel, $1,328; a major, $1,038. Nor could it have been prestige that lured these young men into the army. Rarely in our history have army officers been highly regarded, and this was never more true than in the 1830s.

Thomas Jefferson once said that America could never have a large army, for there would not be enough paupers in the country to fill its enlisted ranks, and our nineteenth-century military forces tended to prove him right. Paid only six dollars a month, they were, except during the periods of economic recession, generally a hard-bitten lot. Drunks, fugitives, and other men unable to adjust to society made up almost half of the enlisted roll, while the balance was composed almost entirely of recently arrived non-English-speaking emigrants using the army to help them adjust to their new environment.

The weaponry of the American Army has generally been inferior to that of its enemies, and that was especially true during the Seminole War. The principal weapon upon which the soldiers relied was the muzzle-loading flintlock musket, obsolete even in the 1830s. As the war progressed, the army used some

47

Model 1819 Hall rifles, a considerable improvement, for they allowed a man to get off four shots without reloading. Unfortunately, as Mahon notes, the Hall rifle had a ". . . mule-like kick [which] often broke the stock, its breechblock leaked vital powder and gas, and it fouled so badly after a few shots as to become almost frozen into position."[2] The Seminole were armed with effective, small-bore, Spanish-made rifles imported from Cuba.

The primary weakness of the American Army in 1835 was not, however, the caliber of its soldiers or its weaponry, but rather its size, for it totaled only 6,758 enlisted men. Divided into one regiment of dragoons (749 men), four of artillery (2,180 men), and seven of infantry (3,829 men), it was expected to garrison some sixty posts throughout the country. The Seminole War was to place a considerable strain on its resources.

Nor was the navy numerically in much better shape. With 746 officers and 4,800 gobs and with a marine corps of 68 officers and 1,350 enlisted men, it manned nineteen ships and numerous shore installations. The West Indies Squadron, composed of a brig and four sloops of war under the command of Captain Alexander J. Dallas, was to make the American Navy's only contribution to the many Indian Wars in which the nation engaged.

In Washington—in fact, throughout the country—there was little doubt that the Seminole would soon be brought to bay. After all, the enemy were only unlettered savages—the conflict would be but a short "police action."

Overconfident and ill-prepared, the nation went to war.

CHAPTER V

Florida

The poorest country two people ever
quarreled over . . .

SURGEON JACOB RHETT MOTTE, 1837

The Territory of Florida in 1835 was divided into three
main parts. West Florida, similar in climate and geography to Alabama, extended from the Perdido River to the Apalachicola River; Middle Florida comprised the area as far east as
the Suwannee and included the capital of Tallahassee; and the
rest of the Territory, down to Key West, was broadly called
East Florida.

In the census of 1830, the Territorial population, not including the Seminole and their Negroes, numbered some 34,730
persons, including 18,000 whites and 16,000 Negro slaves, most
of the latter brought there since the acquisition of Florida by the
United States in 1821. In the thirties, East Florida, the most
sparsely populated of the three areas, remained under the
Americans.

Tallahassee, built in 1824, stood on an elevation a few miles

49

east of the Ochlockonee River, the site of a former Indian village. Almost from its start, the town could boast society as sophisticated as that of other, larger southern cities.*

By 1835 Tallahassee was a vigorous community with a population of 1,500 people, two churches, a jail, and a partially finished Capitol. A naval officer, Captain William Chandler, in a letter to a cousin, described the town as he had seen it in 1836:

> . . . a very pleasant little city, of not many handsome, but substantial and comfortable houses of brick and frame, besides some churches;—built round a knoll and surrounded by dense hammocks, through which diverged roads like the spokes of a wheel. But I remember more particularly the agreeable society, and the beauty of some of the young ladies.[1]

The governor, appointed by the President of the United States at a yearly salary of $2,500, resided in the Territorial capital. There also met the legislature, a unicameral body called the Legislative Council, which since 1826 had been elected by the people of the Territory. A Federal district judge appointed by the President presided in Tallahassee, but local county jurists were appointed by the governor with the consent of the Council.

Besides being the Territorial seat of government, Tallahassee had another distinction. It was connected with its port town of St. Marks by a railroad. The cars were pulled by mules over twenty-four miles of rough track. Constructed in 1834, it was

---

* Achille Murat, the former Prince Royal of the Two Sicilies, settled in 1824 on a large plantation, "Lirona," near Tallahassee. There he acquired a wife, Catherine Willis Grey, a grandniece of George Washington. "The ladies at the large dinner parties frequently held in the homes of the town," he wrote, "are as beautiful and as well dressed as any in New York." After a visit to Tallahassee, a notation in his diary read, "No news in town except a wine party, or rather, eating, drinking, card playing, and segar [sic] smoking."

one of the earliest railroads in the United States, and some said, "one of the worst."[2] There had originally been an engine but it ". . . ran down a bank, twenty feet, and was totally unfit for service."[3] The railroad trip between the two towns took about five hours.

St. Marks, constructed on low marshy land, was a rough frontier town. There were no churches, but probably more taverns per inhabitant than anywhere else in the United States. The houses were small and, as described by visitors, "mean." Unfortunately the water of the Gulf off the town was shallow, and ships of any size had to anchor some eighteen miles away, carrying passengers and freight by lighter.

During the latter part of the Seminole War, the town of Port Leon sprang up three miles below St. Marks. Consisting of about twenty small shacks, it was mainly a transshipment point for cotton bound north from Tallahassee.

All three towns—Tallahassee, St. Marks, and Port Leon— were health hazards. Almost every summer there would be epidemics of "the fever." In 1840 it was reported that out of Tallahassee's population of 1,600 approximately 45 died, and that "almost every one was sick and the only way they kept alive was by taking Calomel by the ounces and now they look like walking skeletons more than like live people."[4]

Besides the capital and its ports, in the thirties there were a number of other important towns in the Territory. Mostly of Spanish origin, they were grouped along the coast or on rivers. St. Augustine was the best known and largest of these towns. The most civilized—in fact, the oldest city in the United States— it was originally settled in 1565. With the possible exception of Tampa, it was nearer the scenes of violence and more involved in the Seminole War than any of the large towns of Florida. At the time its population numbered some 1,700 people, including 1,000 whites, 570 slaves, and 150 free people of color. Its Caucasians were divided into "the old Floridians," those of Spanish or Minorcan descent; the Americans; and a scattering of British subjects. The town still preserved its Latin flavor, with its narrow, winding streets.

Most of the troops in St. Augustine were quartered at St. Francis barracks, in the southern end of the town. Built on an elevation, on the site of a former convent, the building afforded a commanding view of the city.

Socially, St. Augustine became an oasis to the lonely soldiers from the North. There was a series of dinner parties and dances in a town hotel and in private homes as well.

South of St. Augustine and east of St. Johns River, a number of the more substantial men of the city had established large sugar plantations. Worked by slaves, the plantations had proven extremely profitable. On the flatlands, the imposing manor houses and mills could be seen for miles above the verdant growth.

The men and women who clustered around Fort Brooke and who were the founders of Tampa were not the first settlers on the Gulf coast of East Florida. Although fishermen had been exporting dried and salt fish from the Gulf since the early days of Florida's exploration, it was not until the second occupation of Florida by the Spaniards, in 1783, that they established any permanent villages.[5]

As early as 1817 a few settlers had established themselves in the Cedar Keys in the Gulf of Mexico, about halfway between Tampa and St. Marks. In addition to the British traders Alexander Arbuthnot and Robert Ambrister, who made the village on Wey Key their base, there were also settlers on nearby Seahorse Key. The Cedar Keys were said to be the healthiest spot in Florida.

Far to the north in West Florida and almost at the Alabama border was the port city of Pensacola. With its good harbor, it was an extensively used shipping center.

Under Spanish rule settlers had clung to the coastal areas, but after acquisition of the Territory by the United States, new arrivals began a penetration of the interior, and small inland towns began to spring up. Most of them were primitive and, as described by army officers, mean little villages.

The oldest of these hamlets was Micanopy, small, rough and primitive, in central East Florida, about sixty miles southwest of St. Augustine, in the heart of the Indian country.

Perhaps more representative of these new towns was Newnansville, directly west of St. Augustine. Newnansville, in spite of its rough appearance, nevertheless had a social life— mostly centered in its taverns. There were almost nightly balls at which the "double trouble" was danced to the scraping of a fiddle.

Most of the settlers who arrived in Florida after 1821 were unsuccessful small farmers from Georgia, Alabama, and Tennessee. Called "crackers," they were heartily disliked by the army officers, and they reciprocated the feeling. They were individualists who refused to accept any form of discipline, and they made poor citizen-soldiers. The military, including General Jackson, stigmatized them as cowards, which they were not; they in turn considered the Regulars to be snooty, aloof martinets, inefficient "popinjays" from the North, who just didn't know how to fight Indians. Conflict between the Regulars and the militiamen continued throughout the entire Seminole War.

There was considerable justification for the regular officers' low opinion of many settlers. A cracker was often satisfied to clear a small tract, erect a one-room, dirt-floor cabin, and spend the rest of his life fishing, and making and drinking whiskey. The drudgery was left to his woman, who also regularly produced a child a year. To the idealistic graduates of West Point many of the settlers did not appear as sterling examples of manhood.

Not all of the crackers, on the other hand, found existence in the Territory idyllic. The summer heat, the insects, and the snakes at times made life unbearable. One disappointed settler reported that his land produced forty bushels of frogs to the acre and alligators sufficient in numbers to be fenced.

Nor were the crackers the sole reason for the unpopularity of the War among the officers and enlisted men of both the army and the navy. Many of them understood the primary factors that had brought about the War and were not happy at being called upon to fight for the institution of slavery. A number had admiration and sympathy for the Seminole and were not at all reticent about their opinions. A large group, mostly those who came from north of the Mason-Dixon line, considered the conflict a "dirty little war of aggression."

The climate and geography of the Territory were additional enemies of an already burdened fighting man. Florida, particularly during the summer season, was an unhealthy place. More soldiers died there from disease than from enemy bullets. It was common at the inland posts to have half the garrison down with "the fever," which we now know as malaria, during June, July, and August.

The heat during the summer months was intolerable. Often the thermometer would register well over a hundred degrees. And the impossibility of marching infantry any distance over the burning sands made the heavy use of horses necessary.

Poisonous snakes, alligators, scorpions, and hordes of insects also contributed to the unpopularity of campaigning in Florida. Clouds of mosquitoes and gnats were the constant companions of the men. Although medical records do not disclose the number of snake or scorpion bites treated, we know the reptiles and arachnids were greatly feared by the men from the North.

It was, however, the geography of Florida that was most hated by the soldiers. On the highlands the sword palmetto tore at their shoes, clothing, and skin. In the swampy areas, soldiers marched for hours in dank water that often came up to their waists. At night the exhausted men fell down in soggy, dripping clothing, to rest on damp or wet sand.

Assistant Surgeon Motte summed up the Florida situation:

A most hideous region to live in, a perfect paradise for Indians, alligators, serpents, frogs and every other kind of loathsome reptile.

CHAPTER VI

Moultrie Creek

These Indians [the Seminole] can have
no claim to lands in Florida, humanity and
justice is sufficiently extended to them by . . .
permission to return [to Georgia], and live in
peace with their own nation [the Creek].

ANDREW JACKSON, 1821

As the third decade of the nineteenth century dawned, the
situation of the Seminole Nation was almost desperate.
The long struggle with the Americans, lasting from even before
the War of 1812 to the Spanish cession of Florida to the United
States, had ended the relatively affluent life the Indians had
briefly known. Now many of their towns were blackened ruins,
and many of their people were nomads. Their fighting strength,
dissipated in the First Seminole War and later battles, now
seemed only a memory. The vast cattle herds that once grazed
their lands were gone, and they had failed to plant the food
crops that might have sustained them. Hunger and misery had
become a way of life. There remained, however, one more blow
to the pride they had once known.

Andrew Jackson, the Border Captain, the implacable foe of
the Seminole, the man who considered anyone who was not

white to be subhuman, was named the first American Governor of Florida.

There was nothing that the government could have done that would have engendered more restlessness on the part of the Seminole than the naming of Jackson to such a post. It confirmed the worst fears of the Indian leaders: the future would be even more dismal than the past. To those in Washington, this did not seem overly important. When Florida had been bought, the Seminole had "come with the land," and while they were an annoyance, this was a problem that could and would be solved.

Jackson was not happy with the appointment. At first he declined it, but he later relented. He received his commission in March 1821 and arrived in Florida in July. Fortunately for the Seminole, his tenure as Governor of the Territory of Florida was short. Jackson left Florida for the Hermitage, his home outside of Nashville, in early October, and he never returned.

Jackson had submitted to President Monroe a list of possible Territorial officeholders. He was furious when the President ignored his suggested nominees and named a group of his own choosing. He was particularly angry at the naming of Colonel George Walton, Jr., of Georgia, son of a signer of the Declaration of Independence, as Secretary of West Florida, rather than Richard K. Call, a Jackson protégé.

The general correctly concluded that Walton had been named at the behest of his old enemy, Senator William H. Crawford of Georgia, and he was not at all inclined to hide his annoyance. Writing to John C. Calhoun on July 29, 1821, Jackson told the Senator that he would never admit a Crawford man to his confidence.

Jackson was, fortunately, soon over his peeve. Working closely with the Georgian, he became an admirer, a close friend, and a lifelong correspondent of Walton. When he left Florida he recommended that Walton be named Secretary of the entire Territory.

As Governor of Florida, Jackson continued to press for the return of the Seminole to the Creek Confederation in Georgia, either voluntarily or by force. That a deep hatred existed between the Florida Indians and their northern kin seemed not to bother him. If they could not be sent back, then he favored their being concentrated in northwestern Florida near the Georgia and Alabama borders. There they would be away from the coast and could no longer trade for firearms and ammunition with Cuba.

Rumors continued to circulate as to the position the Seminole would occupy under American rule. Often they were the invention of white traders who exploited the Indians' fears. The Seminole were told that "Andy" Jackson intended to wipe out all Indians, or at the best they would be forced to sell their possessions for a paltry sum and emigrate to arid southern Florida.

By mid-July 1821 Micanopy had become unable to bear this uncertainty. He named two white traders he trusted, Horatio Dexter and Edward M. Wanton, both men of substance, to negotiate a treaty for the tribe with the Americans. Jackson's reaction was in character. He ordered the arrest of both men and let it be known that there would be no treaties with the Indians during his tenure as governor. No longer would the tribes be treated as a nation.

Following Jackson's resignation and departure from Florida, William Worthington, Secretary of East Florida, became acting Governor of that Territory, and Colonel George Walton, Jr., assumed those duties in West Florida.

Richard Call evidently felt no animosity toward Walton over his appointment as Secretary of West Florida, for he wrote to Jackson at the Hermitage that the government was running quite smoothly and that Walton had performed his duties "beyond my expectations."

Not so, however, with Judge Henry M. Brackenridge, a former Philadelphia lawyer and Call's law partner. He wrote Caesar A. Rodney on December 20, 1821, that since Jackson had left he had to do everything for Walton. "His companions," he continued, "are persons of no character, or the subalterns of the army with whom he passes every night over the gaming table—he is in truth an object of universal contempt."

Worthington and Walton were succeeded in April 1822 by William Pope DuVal. DuVal was well known and well liked in Florida. Born in Virginia of Huguenot stock, he left home at an early age and settled in Kentucky. Determined to become an attorney, he read law and in 1804 was admitted to the Kentucky bar. His appointment as Governor of Florida followed his being named a Federal judge by Monroe. DuVal had a likable, fun-loving nature, but was no lightweight. He has been described as having a streak of iron within him.

DuVal's appointment was followed by the naming of Major Gad Humphreys of New York as Indian agent for the Territory. Humphreys, an army officer with thirteen years of military service behind him, though several times passed over for promotion, seems to have been appointed more on a basis of financial need rather than for any ability or experience he could bring to the position.

The Indians were the first major problem of the new governor. If anything, they were in an even worse situation than the previous year. Having again failed to plant their fields for fear the crops would be taken by the whites, they were living on venison and coontie-root flour. Half-starved, the Seminole committed a number of robberies, and several whites were killed. DuVal's reaction was quite different from what Jackson's would have been. Rather than raise a hue and cry, he asked the War Department to increase the Indians' food allowance. On one policy, however, DuVal agreed with Jackson. He favored sending the Seminole north to their Creek relatives. If that was impossible, the next-best solution, he said, was to send them west of the Mississippi River.

In spite of his views on migration, DuVal became extremely unpopular with a large segment of the Floridians. In an effort to protect the Indians from conniving whites, he issued a proclamation forbidding those without a license from purchasing slaves, cattle, horses and hogs from the red men. Whites were also enjoined from settling in the vicinity of Seminole towns.

In September a serious epidemic of yellow fever broke out in western Florida, and Governor DuVal found it necessary to return to Kentucky on personal business. Major Humphreys and his subagent Peter Pelham also were required to be absent from the Territory. It was unfortunate, for a council with the Indians had been called at St. Marks on November 20, and George Walton, who was again Acting Governor—this time of all Florida—had not been briefed on what was to be discussed at the meeting. He had also not been provided with the necessary funds for the arrangements or for the traditional presents to be given to the Indians. A number of Chiefs arrived for the council, but it wasn't until a week later that Thomas Wright, an army paymaster, was named acting negotiator in the emergency. But even he had not been given instructions, and the discussions had to be couched in broad, general terms. Humphreys arrived a month later on Christmas Eve, but with little information on what the government's Seminole policy might be.

There was good reason for this lack of information, for *the Administration had not determined upon a Florida Indian policy.* In his annual message to Congress, President Monroe had recommended that the Seminole be either moved out of Florida or confined to a reservation.

The House of Representatives thereupon appointed a committee headed by Thomas Metcalf of Kentucky to study the matter. A majority of the committee members were quite liberal for their day, and their conclusions shocked not only the people

of Florida but those of Georgia and Alabama as well. The committee was evidently of the opinion that a treaty was more than
just a piece of paper, for it proposed that the Indians of Florida
be accorded the rights of citizens as promised in the treaty with
Spain, and thereafter settled as families on plots of land. "Thus
stimulated, they would be prepared to amalgamate with the
white society." While ignoring the wishes of the Seminole
themselves, the recommendations were far in advance of the
times. The report was shelved.

The Administration, however, finally made up its mind. At
the urging of Joseph M. Hernandez, Territorial Delegate to
Congress from Florida, Secretary of War John C. Calhoun announced in early 1823 that Commissioners were to be appointed
to meet with the Indians and insist that they remove to an area
south of the Charlotte River. If there was insufficient soil for
cultivation there, the Commissioners were to be authorized to
extend the reservation north toward Tampa Bay. The Secretary,
who was confused about his geography, evidently meant Pease
Creek, which empties into Charlotte Harbor. This was quite
different from Jackson's policy. He had suggested that the
Seminole be concentrated in West Florida, in the area of the
Apalachicola River, near the Georgia and Alabama borders.

On April 7, Bernardo Segui of Florida and James Gadsden
of South Carolina were named as Commissioners to treat with
the Indians.* On June 30 Governor DuVal was appointed a
third member of the group.

---

* Bernardo Segui, appointed to represent the Floridians, was a natural-
ized American of Minorcan descent. A much-respected citizen of St.
Augustine, he had lived there since 1777. James Gadsden, remembered today for the Gadsden Purchase, had served in the War of 1812
as a lieutenant of engineers and had been on Jackson's staff during the
1818 invasion of Florida. Although he was still a friend of the General,
his appointment in 1821 as a full colonel was not confirmed by the
Senate. Gadsden, while not named as Chairman of the Commission,
gradually assumed that role.

A meeting with the Indians at Moultrie Creek, a few miles south of St. Augustine, was called for September 5, 1823. During the summer Governor DuVal made a wise move. Subagent Peter Pelham had not returned to Florida, so DuVal named Horatio Dexter in his place. Dexter, regarded highly and trusted by the Indians, was given charge of arrangements for the council. He was also able to induce Micanopy to agree that the Alachua band would be present. Prior to the conference, the Indians gathered a short distance from Moultrie Creek and selected Neamathla,* principal Chief of the Mikasukis, as their spokesman.

On the opening day of the Congress, a number of the citizens of St. Augustine arrived to view the festivities. Among them was an Episcopal priest, the Reverend Joshua Nichols Glenn. In his diary he records his impressions:

> Sat 6th, the treaty with the Florida Indians commenced today. In the morning Capt. Wm Levingston his wife and daughter, Mr and Mrs Streeter and myself went up to Moultry [sic] the place of holding the Treaty in a very comfortable boat— accompanied by many other gentlemen and Ladies in other boats —a little after we landed the Indians came from their Camps to the Commissioners Camp to salute the Commissioners and hold their first talk, this was quite novel—the Indians came in a body with a white flag flying—beating little things Similar to a Drum and Singing a kind of a song and at the end of every apparent verse one of them gave a Shrill hoop—which was succeeded by a loud and universal Scream from them all—in this way they marched up to the Commissioners—when two of them in their birthday Suit and painted all over white with White Sticks in

---

* This was the same Neamathla who in November of 1817 had issued the ultimatum to General Gaines at Fort Scott that precipitated the First Seminole War. He was now, however, a more mature and responsible leader, fully cognizant of the depleted strength of the tribes. Governor DuVal was later to say that Neamathla was "uncommonly capable, bold, violent, restless, unable to submit to a superior, or to endure an equal."

their hands and feathers tied on them—come up to them [the Commissioners] and made many marks on them—then their King, Nehlemathlas [sic] came forward and shook hands and after him all the Chiefs in rotation—after which the King smoked his pipe and then observed that he considered us gentlemen as Fathers and Brethren and the Ladies as Mothers and Sisters the Commissioners then conducted the chiefs into the bark house they had built to hold their talks in and after they had all smoked together they held their first talk—in the evening we returned to town . . .[1]

Colonel Gadsden acted as spokesman for the Commissioners. He first justified Jackson's invasion of Florida, and detailed the events that had made such an expedition necessary. He praised the General's forbearance in not driving his enemy into the sea. He assured the Chiefs, however, of the Great White Father's willingness to forgive, provided the Seminole agreed to remove to within a specified area. He ended his peroration with a scarcely veiled threat that if the Indians failed to comply they could only await the dire consequences.

Neamathla spoke for the tribes. At first he was adamant, but after additional threats from Commissioner Gadsden he consented to a concentration of the tribes, but pleaded that they not be sent to the barren and sandy South.

After two weeks of threats on the part of the Commissioners and humble pleas by the Indians, a treaty was agreed upon. It provided that the Seminole would give up all claim to the whole Territory of Florida. They would be confined to an area (as later enlarged) of approximately 4,000,000 acres. The Chiefs had, however, persuaded the Commissioners that they should not be required to go south of Pease Creek. The reservation was to cover an area at least twenty miles from each coast, and extend from Charlotte Harbor on the North to south of Tampa Bay.

The treaty also stipulated that, should the area assigned the Indians not include enough tillable soil, the reservation would be enlarged, and it was later twice so extended. White men, unless authorized, were to be kept off Indian lands. The government would provide an annuity of $5,000 a year for twenty years, $6,000 worth of agricultural equipment, $4,500 for improvements, $2,000 for transportation, $1,000 yearly for twenty years for a school, and $1,000 a year over the same period for a blacksmith and gunsmith.

More important, *the Seminole agreed to discourage runaway slaves from seeking asylum on the reservation.*

In an obvious bribe to certain of the principal Chiefs for signing the treaty, small reservations of from two to eight square miles in the valley of the Apalachicola River were allotted to Neamathla, Blunt, Tuskihadjo, Mulatto King, Emathlochee, and Econchatomico. The Commissioners reported to the Secretary of War that these Chiefs would not have signed the treaty had not such a clause been included.

However, considering the treachery, hypocrisy, and fraud that was to be perpetrated by the white man—soldier, statesman, civilian—against the Seminole during the coming decade, it is no wonder that the red man would begin to gird himself for a final stand.

CHAPTER VII

The Gathering Clouds

> There remains nothing worth words. If the
> hail rattles, let the flowers be crushed . . . the
> stately oak of the forest will lift its head to the
> sky and the storm, towering and unscathed.
>
> OSCEOLA, 1834

Securing an agreement that would confine the Indians to a reservation and actually inducing them to move there are two separate and distinct actions. Certainly there was no rush on the part of the Seminole to go to their new home. By July 1824, only 1,500 had made the move.

DuVal and Gadsden traveled among the Indians in an attempt to persuade them to comply with the terms of the Treaty of Moultrie Creek, but their efforts proved fruitless. Both men reluctantly came to the conclusion that the bulk of the Indians would not move without a show of military force on the part of the United States. "They will not go," Gadsden wrote Secretary of War Calhoun, "unless the United States shows a disposition to compel obedience." He suggested that a fort be established on Tampa Bay.

On November 5, 1823, Lieutenant Colonel George M.

Brooke was ordered to proceed with four companies of the Fourth Infantry to Tampa Bay and establish a military post there. Brooke left Pensacola with his four companies on January 15. At Tampa Bay, they made contact with Colonel Gadsden and his small detachment, who had already made a reconnaissance of the area. They determined the most desirable position for the post to be a site at the juncture of the Hillsborough River and the Bay.*

By letter of April 4, 1824, Colonel Brooke, who had given the new post his own name, reported that by the middle of the next month the men would be in their barracks, the officers' quarters constructed, and the quartermaster's warehouse, the commissary, and the bakehouse built.

The army transport *Florida* arrived periodically at Fort Brooke from Pensacola. The *Florida* carried inspecting parties, supplies, ordnance, officers' wives and frontier-bound civilians. It anchored in the deep water in the bay, and lighters carried the passengers and supplies across the shallow water to the wharf.[1]

In spite of visitors from the outside world, the post was nevertheless a lonely spot for the enlisted personnel. They were permitted to fish and hunt, but beyond that, there was little recreation. There was a Fourth of July celebration with many long speeches in 1824, and on occasion there was a horse race, on which the men were permitted to wager their meager earnings. This was not, however, enough to take care of the excess energy of the troops, many of whom were in their late teens and early

---

* The land had already been cleared and a house and wharf erected by a New Yorker, Robert Hackley. The young man had been under the misapprehension that the land belonged to his father, but the title had been based on a Spanish grant that had been nullified by the subsequent Adams-Onis Treaty. When the troops arrived, Hackley was in Pensacola, where he had gone for supplies. On his return he was dumbfounded to find his plantation in possession of the army. Neither he nor his family was ever able to secure compensation from the government for the improvements he had made.

66

twenties. A few of the men thought up ingenious ways to amuse themselves, such as those who in 1831 published a one-copy, hand-printed newspaper. For the vast majority, boredom was their constant companion, and morale was low. There were constant infractions of regulations, and desertions seemed only to increase as time slowly passed. In 1825, out of a total of 130 men present for duty, twenty-six men were under arrest or in confinement.

It was not long after the post was established that a village, Tampa, began to take form on lands adjacent to the fort. In 1828 William G. Saunders from Mobile, Alabama, established a general store. His was followed by other commercial establishments, including a boatyard, a shoemaker, a boardinghouse, a saloon, and of course the inevitable whorehouse. In 1834, when Hillsborough County was organized, Tampa became the county seat.

The establishment of Fort Brooke did not seem to have the desired effect upon the Indians. Led by Neamathla, the tribes not only seemed unwilling to leave for the reservation, but were sullen and appeared to be on the verge of an outbreak of violence. When word came in July 1824 that an uprising seemed likely and that a large group of warriors had gathered at Neamathla's town, the governor took action. Going to the village with only an interpreter, he gave the warriors a dressing down. They had to meet at St. Marks on July 26, he said, or "face destruction." It took considerable courage on the part of DuVal to face the sullen warriors.

At the St. Marks meeting, where six hundred warriors assembled on July 26, Governor DuVal was not to be placated. He arbitrarily removed Neamathla as principal Chief of the Seminole west of the Suwanee River, and had much to do with the naming of Tuckose Emathla, or John Hicks, as he was called by the whites, as his successor. Fitted for the post not only by his hereditary background but by ability, he was to remain

1837 Lithograph

y James & Gray

Chief, and Neamathla gradually faded into the background. DuVal's arbitrary interference in the internal affairs of the Seminole was accepted with less criticism by the Indians than it was by Secretary of War Calhoun in Washington, and there were ominous grumblings in Congress.

The Indians were less interested in who was their Chief, particularly when the deposed one had made his mark on the Treaty of Moultrie Creek, than they were in ways and means of avoiding a move to the reservation. Attached to the land they had known, they understandably did not want to emigrate south.

Dislike of the Moultrie Creek Treaty and opposition to the insistence that they go to the reservation resulted in a growing resistance on the part of the Indians. Raids on the settlers' cattle herds increased, and there were rumors that a number of the warriors were calling for war on the whites. Colonel Brooke at Tampa Bay noted the unrest, and on April 4, 1824, he wrote to his superiors:

> The Indians appear to me, to be more and more displeased at the treaty, and I am not unapprehensive of some difficulty. . . . There is one absolute necessity, of some field pieces here into the field and I beg, that the Commanding Officer at Pensacola may be directed to have transported to this place, two six pounders, with a proper supply of ammunition and implements.

Indian agent Gad Humphreys did not give much help to those charged with the Indian removal. He openly expressed his opinion that the treaty had been a mistake and that it was unwise to move the Indians too hastily. Finally washing his hands of the whole matter, and without informing the Governor, he took off for the North.

Governor DuVal also had considerable sympathy for the Indians' love of their land, ". . . of their delightful Country," but he knew it was not the time to temporize. Calling out the militia, he assembled a considerable army at Pensacola. His show of force had the desired effect: the Indians west of the Suwanee River again agreed to move to the reservation by October 1, 1824. The administrative problem of so vast a migration, plus the Indians' tendency to drag their feet, caused that date to come and go with a majority of the Seminole still off their reservation.

Meanwhile there was to be a revision in the northern line of the reservation. The Seminole and a number of whites, including the Governor and the Secretary of the Territory, insisted that there was not enough arable land to sustain the Indians within the area allotted. Ten days before leaving office President Monroe approved the inclusion of Big Hammock within the reservation. Agitation for the enlargement of the Indian lands did not, however, end there. Pleas were heard for the inclusion of Big Swamp, which totaled some 6,000 acres of supposedly cultivatable soil. In late December 1825, the new President, John Quincy Adams, included Big Swamp in the Indian lands on a temporary basis. Even so, the following year Governor DuVal, after a thirteen-day trip over the reservation, reported that he had not seen 300 acres of good land. He wrote:

> Nineteen-twentieths of their whole country within the present boundary is by far the poorest and most miserable region I ever beheld.

Adding to the other problems of Indian migrations, 1825 was a year of drought, during which some of the Seminole actually starved to death. The acute period occurred while DuVal was north and George Walton was again Acting Governor. The Indians, searching for food, left their reservation and killed the white settlers' cattle. There was a sharp skirmish in Cabbage Swamp between Indians and a group of whites led by a settler named Solano. When George Walton accused Solano of being

71

the instigator of the fight, Walton was charged with being an Indian-lover. For once, Walton and Humphreys, who did not generally agree, saw eye to eye. They were able to persuade Washington to allot $7,000 for additional rations for the Indians.

There were other causes of friction between the whites, their Territorial government, and the Seminole. Through contact with the Spanish fishermen along the Gulf coast, the Indians continued their trade with Cuba. The Cubans also did not miss the opportunity of plying their trade when DuVal, in the lean years of 1826–1827, permitted the Seminole to go to the coast to fish. Colonel Brooke suggested that he be allowed to block this avenue of trade by the use of force, but while both DuVal and Humphreys were opposed to the trade, the soldier's proposal was ignored.

The fugitive slaves were a continuing source of irritation. The Seminole still gave them asylum, permitting them to remain on Indian lands. There were constant wrangles over Negroes between whites and Indians, and considerable hard feeling was engendered. The slaveholders accused agent Humphreys of refusing to enforce the Territorial Slave Code. Almost as if to confuse the situation, the Seminole began demanding that the government return all Negroes that had been taken by white slave catchers.

Indian-white relations had reached a low point by the spring of 1826, and it was agreed that it would be wise to send a delegation of Chiefs to Washington. It was hoped that they would be impressed with the strength of the whites. John Hicks, Neamathla, Itcho Tustenuggee, Micanopy, Holato Mico, Tulce Emathla, and Fuche Loste Hadjo, as well as the Negro Abraham as interpreter, made the trip. In Washington the Chiefs, speaking through John Hicks, asked that the Big Swamp be permanently added to the Indian lands, that slaves taken by white men be returned, and that talk of schools for Indian edu-

72

Tulcee-Mathla, 1843 lithograph by Rice & Clark

Itcho-Tustinnuggee, 1843 lithograph by Rice & Clark

cation be ended. The Great Spirit, they said, had not intended that Indians should learn to read and write. Finally, they asked that the tribes not be asked again to move, particularly to the West. It was then that John Hicks uttered those famous, almost breathless words. "Here [in Florida] our navel strings were first cut, and the blood from them sank into the earth and made the country dear to us."

The government had long wanted a single leader of the Florida Indians with whom they could deal. Shortly after the return of the Chiefs from Washington, Indian agent Humphreys called the tribes together for an election of a principal Chief of all Seminole. The election was held at the agency, two miles west of Silver Springs. There were two candidates: John Hicks was supported by the Mikasukis and Tallahassees, and Micanopy by the Alachua and their affiliated bands. To keep order, Colonel Brooke sent two companies, under the command of Lieutenant George A. McCall. It was said that three thousand Indians were present. John Hicks was elected, and after ceremonies that included a rattlesnake dance, the new Supreme Chief of the Seminole Nation was installed in his office.

The year 1827 brought another drought. The Indians were again close to starvation, and depredations continued. Settlers' cattle were stolen, and the murders of a number of whites were reported. Governor DuVal issued a proclamation calling out the militia of five counties, but since the men were afraid to leave their homes unprotected, there was little response on the part of the citizen-soldiers. The newly established Division of Indian Affairs of the War Department finally came to the rescue, and Commissioner Thomas L. McKenney allotted $20,000 to relieve the Seminole suffering.

The War Department also took another step that was long overdue. On January 4, 1827, in an effort to centralize military authority in Florida, it named Colonel Duncan L. Clinch overall military Commander in the Territory. Born in North Carolina

General Duncan L. Clinch

in 1787, Clinch was a veteran of the War of 1812. He had entered the Army in 1808 on a direct commission, and by 1819 had become a full colonel. Tall and muscular, Clinch, who weighed over 250 pounds, was indeed an imposing figure. His finely chiseled face appeared austere, but he held the reputation of being both kind to his enlisted men and considerate of his junior officers. He was also known to have considerable sympathy for the Indians, believing that many atrocities had been committed by a small number of renegades and that most of the Seminole were peacefully inclined. With an eye toward eventual retirement from the Army, he established plantations in both Georgia and Florida, and he wasn't at all reluctant to use his military position to protect his properties.

Besides his Fourth Infantry Regiment, Clinch's forces in Florida at the time of his appointment included a battalion of the First Infantry Regiment at Pensacola and one company of the Fourth Artillery at St. Augustine. Later he deployed his troops with two companies of the Fourth at Fort Brooke and the Artillery at St. Augustine, and kept four companies in reserve at Pensacola. In early 1827 he also directed the building of Cantonment King, later called Fort King, near the Indian agency at Silver Springs. Major General Alexander Macomb, who had become Commanding General of the Army in 1828, ordered— over Colonel Clinch's protest—that Cantonment King be abandoned. He maintained it was too expensive for the army to bring supplies overland from Tampa Bay. Evidently he changed his mind, for in 1832 the post was reactivated, this time as Fort King.

In 1829, when Lieutenant Colonel Brooke was transferred from the Territory, Colonel Clinch moved his headquarters and the remaining companies of the Fourth Infantry to Fort Brooke. It was there that Clinch learned that he had received the brevet of brigadier general.

CHAPTER VIII

Paynes' Landing
and Fort Gibson

[The Treaty of Paynes' Landing was] a
foul blot upon the the escutcheon of the nation.

THOMAS L. MCKENNEY, 1835[1]

T he white Floridians were bitterly anti-Indian. Most of
them firmly believed that "the only good Indian was a
dead Indian."[2] Almost to a man, they favored either the
Seminole's removal to Arkansas or Oklahoma, or their annihilation. In early January of 1827, the Legislative Council passed
an act directed at the Seminole, providing the death penalty for
anyone aiding a slave to escape. Later the same month a bill was
approved to ". . . prevent the Indians from roaming at large
through the Territory." It provided that any citizen who found
an Indian off the reservation might take him to the nearest
justice of the peace, who could confiscate his gun and sentence
him to thirty lashes.

By 1832 the movement for emigration west had crystallized,
and in April of that year the Council endorsed that policy in a
petition to Congress. The Council's action was followed by a

number of similar petitions to Congress from the towns and counties of Florida.

While Governor DuVal had originally been a moderate on the Indian question, he gradually swung to the right and favored the policy of migration. Not so, however, the Indian agent Gad Humphreys, a staunch friend of his Seminole wards. For his stand, he was ultimately to become the favorite whipping boy of the Florida whites. He was charged by the owners of fugitives of not aiding in the capture of their runaways, of being dilatory in turning over to their masters the few slaves that the Indians sent him, and of using these Negroes for work on his own plantation before restoring them to their white owners. The accusations against Humphreys finally reached President John Quincy Adams. He named Alexander Adair to go to Florida and investigate the charges. Hearings were held in St. Augustine, and although Humphreys admitted that he was opposed to the government's policy of endeavoring to secure the return of slaves, the meetings produced no proof of his guilt as charged.

As time would show, however, the Florida settlers were not finished. In 1831, after Jackson became President, Governor DuVal joined the group against Humphreys. He recommended to the President that the agent and a certain Judge Joseph L. Smith, who had handed down a decision that Indian annuities could not be withheld, be removed from office. James Gadsden and Joseph M. White, a leading citizen and the third Territorial delegate to Congress, joined with DuVal against Humphreys. In 1831 President Jackson removed Humphreys and named Indian subagent John Phagan in his place. Humphreys retired to a small trading post near the reservation.

By today's standards, Andrew Jackson was a racist. A man of personal violence, he did not object to the use of force in dealing with those of another race or nationality. On January 30, 1832, Jackson's good friend James Gadsden, now a resident of Flor-

79

ida, was named as a special agent to negotiate with the Seminole for their voluntary removal west of the Mississippi. Jackson, who was facing a reelection campaign, thus not only appeased the demands of the Florida settlers but made the proposed move voluntary, in order not to antagonize the considerable pro-Indian block in the northeastern states.

Though they were kin of the Seminole, the Creek had fought on the side of the Americans in each of the invasions of Florida since before the War of 1812. Furthermore, seeking slaves to sell to the whites, they had long followed a policy of raiding Seminole towns and taking back to Georgia any Negroes they found. Jackson's determination to return the Seminole to Creek domination did not make the problems of James Gadsden any easier.

This time Gadsden selected Paynes' Landing on the Oklawaha River, in central Florida, as the site of his council. However, it was not until early May 1832 that a sufficient number of the Chiefs had gathered to begin the talks.

What actually occurred at Paynes' Landing has long been shrouded in mystery. Not only were there no minutes kept of the proceedings, but contemporary accounts differ wildly. All we do know for certain is that a treaty was produced and that it appears to bear the marks of seven principal Chiefs and eight sub-Chiefs. However, a number of the senior Chiefs, including Micanopy, denied that they had made their mark on the instrument. Others of the Indians, Charley Emathla for one, later claimed that the whites used force to obtain their consent to the agreement.

An army officer, Major Ethan Allen Hitchcock, who was not at the scene, but who claimed that he had interviewed many of the participants, insisted that the treaty was tainted with fraud and that Abraham had been given a $200 bribe to misinterpret. His authority, he said, was Captain Charles M. Thruston, who stated that he had been present when Gadsden told President

Jackson that Indian concurrence to the treaty could not have
been procured without such a bribe. Certainly Abraham's conduct both before and during the conflict that followed the meeting belies this charge, and yet both Hitchcock and Thruston
were apparently honest men. It is hard to believe that their
stories were mere inventions. It is also truly difficult to understand why, if the Chiefs' marks were genuine and there was no
coercion or bribe, they would ever have signed an agreement
with terms as onerous as those of Paynes' Landing.

The treaty, it was later charged, was drawn up in Washington and sent to Gadsden to secure Indian approval. However, if
it was drawn up by a lawyer, he was one with scant legal
training. Its wording, in part, was so ambiguous that it could
only be the subject of later controversy.

The preamble provided that the Indians were willing that a
delegation of their Chiefs should travel to the West to inspect
the Creek lands, and "should they be satisfied with the character
of that country, and of the favorable disposition of the Creeks to
reunite with the Seminole as one people, the treaty would be
binding." Indians and some white men contended that the word
"they" referred to the whole Seminole Nation. The government and most whites insisted that "they" referred to the delegation sent west. Lewis Cass at first said, in his 1832 report as
Secretary of War to the President, arguing that a move to the
West was voluntary on the part of the Seminole, "The treaty,
however, is not obligatory on their [the Indians'] part until a
deputation sent by them shall have examined the country proposed for their residence, and until the tribe, upon their report,
shall have signified their desire to embrace the terms of the
treaty." Cass was to change his mind later.

Should the treaty become binding as the result of a favorable
report on the part of the Chiefs who were to visit the West—
and, the Indians contended, a favorable conclusion on the part of
the whole Seminole Nation—the Indians agreed to remove to

their new home within three years after such ratification, a third of the tribes going each year. Grants to be paid by the government totaled approximately $80,000, or about two cents an acre for the 4,032,940 acres granted the Seminole under the Treaty of Moultrie Creek.

When the terms of the Treaty of Paynes' Landing became known, it received the warm approbation of the Florida settlers. It not only freed them from the menace of the "savage" and their Negro protégés, but it also opened up a vast territory for settlement. Others were not so enthusiastic. The treaty was opposed almost unanimously by the army officers serving in Florida, many of whom were sympathetic to the Indians' cause,[3] and it was bitterly criticized by the opponents of the Administration.

It was originally planned that the delegation of Chiefs who were to go west under the terms of the treaty would leave in July, after the Green Corn Dance. They did not, however, get away until mid-October, 1832. The group leaving Florida consisted of Jumper, Holato Emathla, his son Charley, Coa Hadjo, Yahadjo, John Hicks, Nehathoclo, and the Negro Abraham. The Indian agent John Phagan accompanied the group. It is doubtful that any of the Indians would have made the trip had they suspected the duplicity that would be practiced and the pressures to which they would be subjected.

In February 1833 Henry L. Ellsworth of Connecticut, the Reverend John F. Schermerhorn of New York, and the Governor of North Carolina, Monfort Stokes, were named Commissioners of Indian Affairs, West, to deal with the Seminole delegation.* They arrived at Fort Gibson, on the Grand River a little above its confluence with the Arkansas.

---

* Jackson had a hard time filling his delegation. Initially, five men had turned down the appointment. Stokes resigned as Governor of North Carolina to accept the new post, and Ellsworth was from a prominent New England family, while Schermerhorn, less well known, was a Dutch Reformed Clergyman.

The Commissioners first turned their efforts toward securing an agreement by the Creek to accept the Seminole as a part of their confederation. On February 14, 1833, a treaty was signed which provided for this and allotted lands on which the Florida Indians would live.

The Seminole Chiefs, while waiting for the Commission, looked over the country. They were not happy with what they saw. The land they were to receive for their Florida holdings was cold, barren and storm-swept. "Snow covers the ground," the Chiefs said, "and frost chills the hearts of men." They continued, "You would send us among bad Indians with whom we could never be at rest. . . . Even our horses were stolen by the Pawnee, and we are obliged to carry our packs on our backs. . . . We are not hungry for other lands. If we are torn from our forests, our heartstrings will snap."

The Indian delegation was told by the Commissioners that, under instructions from the President, they were to sign a new treaty on behalf of the Seminole Nation, providing that the move to the new lands was satisfactory and that the move "to their new home" would commence "as soon as the government makes arrangements for the emigration, satisfactory to the Seminole Nation." Vainly they protested that they were not authorized to speak for their tribes and that they had come west as a fact-finding committee only. Agent Phagan bluntly made the situation clear. If the delegation did not agree to the treaty, they could not return to Florida. They argued, but to no avail. Finally they made their marks on the purported treaty, and the signing was witnessed by Abraham.

The report of the Commission to the President was a masterpiece of hypocrisy. They wrote, "The Seminoles who were referred to the Commissioners for advice and assistance . . . have been well accommodated. This nation is by the late treaty [Fort Gibson], happily united with its kindred friends [the Creeks] and forms with them one nation; but is secured the privilege of a separate location. . . . This tribe, it is expected, will remove immediately to the lands assigned them." As Professor Mahon writes:

> . . . although it cannot be proved by specific documents, I believe that Agent John Phagan prepared the treaty, forced it upon the Indians, and then secured the acquiescence of the commissioners without their bothering to inquire into it. Part of his game was the stipulation in the treaty that he himself should be agent for the Seminole removal. This the Indians swallowed with the rest. He had also, when quoting from the Treaty of Paynes' Landing, altered the words. Considering that Phagan was soon removed from his post for malfeasance the presumption of questionable conduct on his part seems justified.[4]

It is significant that the Treaty of Fort Gibson misquoted the preamble of the Treaty of Paynes' Landing as "should this delegation be satisfied" instead of "should they be satisfied."

Returning to Florida, the delegation of Chiefs found that news of the agreement had preceded them. To most of the Seminole, however, the Treaty of Fort Gibson, having been signed by unauthorized representatives, was a nullity. As Jumper was later to say:

> . . . We went according to agreement and saw the land. It is no doubt good and the fruit of the soil may smell sweet and taste good and be healthy, but it is surrounded by bad and hostile neighbors, and the fruit of bad neighborhood is blood that spoils the land, and fire that dries the brook. When in the West, I told the Agent [John Phagan] "You say our people are rogues, but you would bring us among worse rogues to destroy us." . . . When we saw the land, we said nothing; but the agent of the United States made us sign our hands to a paper which you say signified our consent to remove; but we considered that we did no more than say we liked the land and when we returned the Nation could decide. We had no authority to do more.[5]

84

Osceola added, "The white people got some of our Chiefs to sign a paper to give our lands to them; but our Chiefs did not do as we told them to do. They did wrong. . . ."

Little attention in Washington, however, was paid to the protests of the Indians. President Jackson submitted the treaty to the Senate in March, and on April 8, 1834, it was unanimously approved.

CHAPTER IX

The Storm
Breaks

. . . the miserable creatures [the Seminole]
will be speedily swept from the earth.

Niles Register, 1834

It is not often that men receive retribution for their sins as
promptly as did John Phagan. While he was at Fort Gibson
his accounts were audited. It was found that vouchers had been
raised after being approved by the merchants, the difference
going into the agent's pocket. He was dismissed in disgrace, and
General Wiley Thompson was named in his place.

On April 24, 1834, almost as if to wipe the slate clean and
make a new start in Florida, the President nominated John H.
Eaton as successor to Governor William P. DuVal. Eaton, an
able man, had been a Senator from Tennessee, and Secretary of
War under the Jackson administration.

It was probably during the early 1830s that Micanopy,
Abraham, Osceola and most of the other leaders of the Seminole
Nation concluded that the United States was knowingly follow-
ing a course that could only bring about the destruction of the

86

Seminole. War was inevitable. There were no outright acts of aggression on the part of the Chiefs, and they continued to treat with the whites, but Abraham and John Caesar began making contact with the slaves on the plantations along the St. Johns River. It was noted that at the meeting of the Chiefs convened by agent Thompson on October 21, 1834, to pay what was to be the last annuity in Florida, more of the money went to purchase powder and ball than in the past. The Seminole were preparing themselves for combat.

In the talks that followed, Thompson again tried to make it clear that the question was not whether the Indians wanted to or should move to the West, but rather how the migration should be effected. The Chiefs, for their part, were unusually determined that going beyond the Mississippi was still a subject for discussion. Thompson finally became so exasperated that, on the breakup of the meeting, he refused to give the red men their customary presents.

After the first day of talks at the October 1834 Council, the Seminole gathered for a conference of their own. Spies that Thompson sent to the Indian meeting reported that Osceola favored a united stand against the whites and felt that any Chief who favored migration should be proscribed. This was probably the first time that the attention of the whites had been drawn to the young Red Stick as an emerging Seminole leader. They were to hear much more from him as the months passed.

It was not just the young firebrands who favored resisting the whites with force. Many of the older, more mature Chiefs saw the move west to the lands of the Creek as the end of the Seminole people. And, of course, the Negroes' influence over their supposed masters cannot be discounted. With much justification they feared that they would be seized on the move west and returned to their original state of slavery. Their every effort was accordingly bent on bucking up the Indians' inclination to resist the whites' plan to move them west. Mahon notes that peace seemed to hang on the issue of ". . . the ownership of Indian Negroes."[1]

In March Thompson called another conference to read an address of the President to the Chiefs. This was that memorable meeting when the platform on which the dignitaries were seated collapsed and red and white were thrown together in a writhing mass. When both red and white dignity had been restored, the Great White Father's message was presented. The Indians would have to migrate as they had agreed. The Chiefs asked for and were granted thirty days' grace in which to consider Jackson's words.

The Seminole again assembled on April 22. It was a large gathering, with some 1,500 Indians attending. Word had gone forth that another annuity would be paid. That of October 1834 had, after all, not been the last. It had been a bitterly cold winter, and many of the Indians were near starvation. They were given help, but they paid a high price for it. As stated earlier, sixteen of their Chiefs were forced to sign a paper acknowledging the validity of the Paynes' Landing Treaty. It was then that agent Thompson removed from office the five Chiefs who either refused to sign or were not present.

Following the arrest of Osceola by agent Thompson in June, it was noted that the red men were buying excessive amounts of firearms and ammunition. Thompson therefore forbade further sales. He also ordered that slave catchers or traders be forbidden to enter Indian lands. Both actions were approved in Washington.

Starting in June 1835, as described earlier, a series of acts of violence erupted. Seven white settlers captured five Seminole in Alachua County, off the reservation, and beat them with leather lashes. Two Indians coming to the rescue wounded three of the whites. One Indian was killed and another wounded. The murder in August of Private Kinsley H. Dalton, Third Artillery, a mail courier between Fort Brooke and Fort King, was answered when the War Department ordered four more companies of troops to Florida. And in November Osceola was again heard from, when he shot and killed Charles Emathla, the one Seminole Chief who had consistently supported the whites in their plans for western emigration of the tribes.

The white Florida settlers were now thoroughly aroused, almost panicked. Convinced that the Federal authorities would not take action against these acts of violence, they began measuring their own resources.

Brigadier General Joseph M. Hernandez, Commander of the East Florida Militia, on his own authority called to duty a portion of his command. Hernandez, one of the most respected figures in the Territory, was a Spanish-American who became a citizen of the United States after Spain had ceded Florida. Hernandez had served a term as the Territorial delegate to Congress, starting in 1822. A plantation owner and a merchant, he commanded the Territorial Militia during the entire war.

When General Hernandez began to dispose his forces in an attempt to defend the outlying plantations, he found that not all of his fellow planters considered the proximity of militia troops a blessing. They were afraid that large bodies of such civilian troops nearby might invite Indian attack. They also took a dim view of the fighting potential of the militiamen. At Belowville Plantation the owner fired a cannon toward his proposed defenders, hoping to scare them away. Dunlawton Plantation was forcibly occupied, but only after its owner was inducted into the Militia.

Perhaps there was some sound justification for the low opinion the planters held for the Territorial troops. James Ormond, an orderly sergeant of the Mosquito Roarers, described his outfit as "an undisciplined rabble, under no command of their officers, not a man had ever before seen a gun fired in anger." In January

89

1836 his unit was part of a force under Major Benjamin Putnam, Commanding Officer of the St. Augustine Guards, sent by boat to Dunlawton Plantation on reconnaissance for food. At Ormond, he reported, the buildings were on fire when the troops arrived at the plantation wharf. Nevertheless, they disembarked and "chased chickens" for a while.

That evening they camped near the cattle pen, in the expectation that the Indians would return for beef. Shortly after dawn a lone Seminole made his appearance and was shot. The militiamen scalped and otherwise mutilated his body. Indians opened fire, and the militiamen withdrew toward the protection of the ruined manor house. A half hour later a general retreat toward the river was stopped when a Negro guide called out, "My God, gentlemen, is you going to run from a passel of damn Indians?"

When a militiaman was killed, a second withdrawal soon became a rout. In trying to get into the boat, most of the men allowed their guns to become wet and useless. Two troopers refused to wait their turn and tried to swim across the river. One was captured by the Indians. The other was shot in his rear as he climbed into the boat. Three others were wounded. In the panic, the boat was run aground. Fortunately for the militia, at that point an Indian was shot, and the hostiles took off. Major Putnam reported that "after a brisk engagement, the troops made an orderly withdrawal in the face of a superior force."

Governor Eaton also took action. Four hundred volunteers under the command of Militia Brigadier General Richard Keith Call were enlisted for a four-week tour of duty. Call, a lawyer in Tallahassee, had some military experience. He had previously distinguished himself in the Battle of Horseshoe Bend, where he was noticed by Jackson, and thereafter became a friend and protégé of the general. Given a commission in the Regular army, he subsequently became a captain and served with Jackson in his first Florida expedition. Having taken a liking to the Territory, he resigned from the army, read law in Pensacola, and eventually set up practice there. He made it a point, however, to continue his friendship with Jackson through correspondence.

Call pictured himself as a great military leader. When he was named Brigadier General of the West Florida Militia on Jackson's recommendation, he accepted the appointment with alacrity.

On their short tour of duty, a portion of Call's mounted volunteers took part in what has been called the Battle of Black Point.

Colonel John Warren of the Florida Militia, leading a baggage train along the rim of the Alachua Savannah on December 18, 1835, was attacked by eighty warriors led by Osceola. The Indians readily captured the train. They had been in possession of their booty but a short time when they were discovered by Doctor John McLemore at the head of thirty mounted militiamen. The doctor ordered a charge, but only twelve of his men responded. The white troops were forced to withdraw, with a loss of six dead and eight wounded.[2]

A few days later Call and his men came upon Osceola's warriors camped on a hammock. Call ordered six companies to dismount and charge the Indians. The troops, fighting waist-deep in water and in "half pistol-shot distance," drove off the hostiles. Papers from the wagon train were recovered, but little else. If the engagement at Black Point was, as some writers have called it, the first battle of the (Second) Seminole War, then like the other early actions it was a defeat for the whites.

Starting around Christmastime, the Indians and their Negro allies began their planned attacks on the St. Johns River sugar-producing plantations. General Hernandez did his best to defend the area, but there just were not enough troops. Within a little more than a week the Indians, aided by the revolting plantation slaves, had devastated a swath of fifty miles between the St. Johns and the Suwannee Rivers.

The Dade Massacre and the murder of Wiley Thompson followed. The second Seminole conflict had become a full-scale war.

CHAPTER X

The Battle of
the Withlacoochee

It is . . . hard to excuse the relaxation of
the army just at the time when it was divided
by the river.

JOHN K. MAHON, 1967

Early in December 1835, General Clinch withdrew the
bulk of the troops at Fort King to his four-mile-square
plantation "Auld Lang Syne." What prompted the move,
other than a desire to protect his property, is hard to determine.
It was no closer to the Seminole strongpoint in the cove of
the Withlacoochee River than was Fort King. Certainly its
accommodations were not an improvement, for the enlisted men
occupied the former slave quarters, which were thatched with
reeds and without windows. The men were driven to distraction
by the lice and other marauding insects. However, in fairness to
the general, the new post was twenty miles nearer than Fort
King to the supply point at Micanopy.

Whatever his reasons, the general made the move and put
the swashbuckling Captain Gustavus S. Drane to work building
a stockade and blockhouse. Drane, who claimed that with sixty

men he could march through the entire Seminole Nation, was a rarity—one of the very few officers in the American Army of the early nineteenth century who rose from the ranks. Boastful and vain, he was nevertheless a man of considerable charm and great energy. He and his men set to work and soon threw up a twelve-foot picket wall around the buildings, enclosing an area of about 150 by 80 yards.

Dubbing the new post Fort Drane, in honor of its builder, General Clinch set about gathering together a sufficient force. On Christmas Eve General Call arrived at Fort Drane with 550 of his mounted volunteers. Call was later to claim that he suggested an immediate and rapid move against the Seminole.

Clinch knew of the St. Johns area depredation, but not of the Dade Massacre or the fate of Wiley Thompson. On December 29 his force of 250 Regulars, under Brevet Lieutenant Colonel Alexander C. W. Fanning, and 500 Florida Volunteers, commanded by General Call, moved south toward the Withlacoochee River. Left behind to defend Fort Drane were a company of Regulars and about a hundred men on the sick list.

Held back by their cumbersome wagon train of baggage and the snakelike path that was called a road, General Clinch's command made slow progress. Skirting low hills and swampy hammocks and ponds, they meandered south. At times the path became so narrow and overgrown that "pioneers" with axes had to precede the column, widening the road as they went.

On the night of the second day the troops bivouacked at a spot three miles from the Withlacoochee. The men sat around in small, quiet groups. An English boy, a medical corpsman, wrote in his diary about a friend, Private Fisher:

> . . . The warrant master Fisher, poor kind fellow, lodged with me in a small tent. We had no fire, none being permitted. So we ate our pork and biscuit, feeling rather lonely, although surrounded by many comrades. Fisher gave me freely to understand the state of his feelings. Tomorrow we were to reach the river,

94

and as it was believed the enemy would dispute the crossing, this poor boy was melancholy and full of dread. His forebodings caused him to be terribly afraid of a collision and he passed a sleepless night. The fact of his term of service being nearly expired made him doubly anxious to be in his beloved New York again.[1]

New Year's Eve dawned clear and cold. Contrary to orders, an undisciplined militiaman blew reveille. General Clinch feared that it could be heard for miles. His understandable concern was academic, for the Seminole had been scouting the column for the last twenty-four hours.

Military success is not always the result of careful planning. It is at times the product of pure chance. Three miles above the spot where General Clinch planned to cross the river was a ford of which neither Clinch nor his scouts had knowledge. The Indians, sure that the whites would cross the river there, laid an ambush for the oncoming troops at the ford. There, 230 Seminole and 30 Negro warriors waited quietly in their concealed positions. Thus Clinch, through ignorance or faulty reconnaissance, avoided the trap. Although they were impeded by thick and tangled growth, the troops reached the river bank at about dawn without a shot having been fired.

Through the help of rafts that some of the men built and the swimming ability of a number of others, by one o'clock the Regulars had crossed the river and deployed themselves facing a thick hammock about 400 yards beyond the bank.

Most of the militia were not so prompt in getting across the river, and for a while it looked as if almost all would refuse to cross. The men from Middle Florida were quite open in their refusal to go farther. Their enlistment was to end in about twelve hours, and in the meantime they refused to risk their lives. Some thirty finally did move, but in the direction of Fort Drane. Their enlistment, they said, had expired, and they were going home. Call seemed to have entirely lost control of his

troops, although Clinch, who was always loath to speak ill of any man, later insisted that the militia general did his best.

Word finally reached Osceola and the warriors waiting in ambush that the troops were crossing the river at another point. Led by the young War Chief in a blue officer's coat, a souvenir of the Dade Massacre, the Seminole headed downstream. Between thirty and sixty of the volunteers had finally made the crossing, when Captain Charles Mellon, commanding a company

is Chiefs

of Regulars, spotted the first Indian. The Regulars opened a steady fire and their smooth-bore muskets were answered by the high-quality Spanish-made rifles the Indians had recently acquired from Cuba. General Clinch, still on the north bank, spurred his horse into the water and, on reaching the far bank, galloped toward the sound of the guns. General Call followed.

Meeting Lieutenant Thomas Ridgely, who had been wounded, Clinch ordered him to the aid station that had been set up near the river bank. Clinch, followed by his aide Major John Lytle, continued up to the left side of the line.

Meanwhile, Lieutenant Colonel Fanning formed his troops in double ranks and ordered an advance. They reached the scrub line, where they were temporarily stopped.

Although Lieutenant Colonel Fanning had lost an arm at the Battle of Lake Erie, he had not lost his courage. The slight figure on horseback, waving his sword and shouting encouragement to his men, seemed to be all over the battlefield. An officer was later to write that there was "a soldier of tested courage, and an officer of approved skill—with full experience in . . . savage warfare."

However, both flanks of the Regulars were exposed, and Osceola saw his advantage. If he could turn the enemy right, isolating them from the river crossing, the battle would be his. Between the troops and the river was an area of scrub pines, and it was from there that the blue-coated Indian leader launched his attack.

For a time the war whoops of the savages, the cries of the wounded, and the sharp crack of gunfire made it impossible to determine just what was happening on the field, but the Indians' attack was finally met by the companies of captains Gates and Mellon. A countercharge with fixed bayonets drove the Indians and Negroes back through the scrub. General Clinch hastily sent an order to Call to bring over the volunteers and plug the hole on the right. General Call, who by then had crossed to the south bank, gathered together what militiamen he could find and deployed them in the breach between the Regulars and the river.

While the threat to the right was no longer immediate, the situation of the troops had not greatly improved. The strength of the Indians and their Negro allies had increased, and the whites were now outnumbered three to one. A third of the soldiers had been killed or wounded, and it was clear that the bulk of the volunteers would not leave their safe view of the battle from the north bank. Slowly—almost imperceptibly—and without an order, the Regulars began to withdraw before the steady advance of the red men.

General Clinch was in a desperate position. Gone was any hope of a decisive, quick victory. All he could hope for was to save the rest of his command. He had taken a bullet through his cap, one through his sleeve, and his horse had been shot from beneath him. Shouting encouragement, he took a position forward of his troops and ordered a charge. The command was carried down the line and the men again began to advance. Captain Graham took a ball that shattered his jaw, but refused Clinch's order to go to the rear. Minutes later Graham received a wound in the hip and this time had no choice. A Private Woods received a shot in the side of his head and one in his hip, but continued to advance until he took one in the shoulder. Finally the advancing men reached the protection of the hammock, and the fire eased.

Meanwhile, Colonel Warren and his troops did yeoman duty in protecting the right flank. A group of about a dozen Seminole and Negro warriors who had again infiltrated the area between the Regulars and the river were stopped and driven back. With the right flank safe, the Regulars formed a semicircle, with their right, left, and rear anchored on the river.

On the north bank, the militia had been deployed in a circle, facing north, with both flanks ending on the Withlacoochee. Any thought of supporting the Regulars had long since been abandoned when an order came from General Call that they should stay on the north bank. The reason behind this command has long remained a point of controversy.[2] Charitably, it can be called a strange military order. Not all of the volunteers were idle, however, for without orders from their general they started to build a low bridge of logs across the river.

In the late afternoon, Osceola was wounded. Though not serious, it considerably restricted his movements. Thereafter several half-hearted attempts to penetrate the whites' position were made, but each time the soldiers held and drove back the enemy. It was obvious that to be successful an attack would have to be in full force, which would be extremely costly. As evening approached, the Indians and Negroes accordingly broke off action and silently withdrew. The Battle of the Withlacoochee was over. Clinch withdrew his troops over the bridge the volunteers had thrown up, and the next day he started his march back to Fort Drane.

The whites called the Battle of the Withlacoochee a draw, but the advantage had gone to the Indians. They had stopped and driven north an invasion of their homeland.

The Battle of the Withlacoochee had ended, but the controversy that it invoked would continue. General Clinch was, to say the least, quite charitable. While mildly critical of the volunteers, he praised General Call's conduct with the words:

> Brigadier General Call after using every effort to induce the Volunteers remaining on the East Bank, when the action commenced, to cross the river, and in arranging the troops still remaining on that bank, crossed over and rendered important service by his coolness and judgment in arranging part of his corps on the right of the Regulars, which gave much strength and security to that flank.[3]

Call, however, was not appeased. "The fictitious reputation and vainglorious boasting of this individual [Clinch]," he wrote, "has long excited my mirth." He then proceeded to criticize every step Clinch had taken after leaving Fort Drane.[4]

The Battle of Withlacoochee had been a serious, bloody affair. Though there were only four soldiers killed, fifty-nine had been seriously wounded. The whites, both in Washington and Florida, now knew that the suppression of the Seminole revolt would be a long and hazardous business. They had on their hands not a simple military action, but a war.

CHAPTER XI

"Old Fuss and Feathers"

[Scott] . . . was one of nature's finest
specimens of the genus *Homo,* yet quite un-
suitable for Indian bush fighting.

JOHN BEMROSE, 1860

With a half-dozen wounds, weak from the loss of blood
and crawling the sixty miles from the site of Dade's
Massacre, Private Ransome Clarke had finally and incredibly
reached Fort Brooke on December 29.* The wretched soldier
duly reported to the commanding officer, Captain Belton.

Captain Francis S. Belton, Commander of Fort Brooke, after
hearing the almost incoherent report of the wounded enlisted
man, was to dispatch a sloop to Key West with a call on the navy
for help.

A number of wives and families of officers stationed at
Brooke and at other forts in Florida were at Key West, and
word of the tragedy created a shock in the little fishing town.

---

* He had become separated from Edwin DeCourcy, and the latter had
been discovered and killed by an Indian.[1]

There were no naval vessels in the harbor, however, and the port captain was forced to call on the United States Revenue Cutter *Washington*[2] to go to the assistance of the beleaguered post. Carrying fifty marines, under the command of Lieutenant Waldron, and a number of cannon, the *Washington* was the first ship from the outside world to reach Fort Brooke after the Dade tragedy. The Seminole War had thus become a joint-command operation.

A few additional men, as well as ordnance and supplies, arrived at Brooke by ship from Baton Rouge as soon as the news reached that town. However, the military situation at Fort Brooke and in the rest of Florida was unsteady. With most of its militia in the field trying to guard the St. Johns River plantation, St. Augustine was left with seventy citizen-soldiers who had but thirty-four guns among them. Pensacola, which General Call had drained of militia, was in equally bad straits.

When word of the engagements in Florida, particularly the Battle of Withlacoochee, reached Washington, Congress appropriated a total of $650,000 for the suppression of the Seminole revolt and the War Department directed Brevet Brigadier General Abraham Eustis[3] in Charleston to gather as many troops as he could and march with them to St. Augustine. Three revenue cutters were directed to cooperate with General Clinch, and he was authorized to draw on the arsenals in Augusta, Georgia; Vernon, Alabama; and Charlestown, South Carolina, for arms and equipment. Clinch was also permitted to induct into Federal service as many militia as needed. The War Department revealed the basic cause of the Seminole War in a message to Congress and in orders to Clinch. No terms were to be offered to the Indians as long as one white man's slave remained among the Seminole. Nor, Clinch was told, was he authorized to negotiate with the hostiles. They had to be reduced to a state of unconditional surrender.

Five days after Washington learned of the Battle of Withlacoochee, the War Department indicated how serious it considered the situation, by ordering General Winfield Scott to assume command in Florida. The general ranked among the greatest military leaders in America. Six foot four, heavily built, and with a commanding presence, he looked the part of the nineteenth-century soldier. Born in Virginia in 1785, Scott was a veteran of the War of 1812, in which he had been one of the very few able field commanders. By 1814 he had become a brigadier general. A lover of all things martial, Scott reveled in uniforms, bugle calls, and the ceremonies of the military. Wherever he traveled he took with him a large staff and a band. His tent in the field was furnished with rugs, chairs, and a bed, and his mess always served the proper wines and liquors. Later, during the Mexican War, he was to be known among his men as "Old Fuss and Feathers."

Besides his devotion to good living and military pomp, Scott had other characteristics seemingly in conflict with his reputation as a great military leader. Whenever he wrote or made a speech, he was likely to "put his foot in his mouth." He was also overly inclined to adhere too rigidly to the book, unwise for an officer engaged in non-European warfare. He was inclined to insist that men fighting in the semi-tropics observe the military courtesies and wear the conventional heavy woolen uniform.

While Scott had his admirers, no man of his stamp could be without a full quota of enemies. Perhaps the foremost of those who took a dim view of the general was Major General Edmund Pendleton Gaines, Commander of the Western Department, with headquarters at New Orleans. Scott's commission as colonel and Gaines' commission as brigadier general bore the same date, and neither man was inclined to give an inch to the other.

Understandably, Gaines had long wanted to command an army in the field. Three years earlier, his chance had come, when the Black Hawk War erupted within the area of his com-

General Winfield Scott

mand. Andy Jackson had not seen it that way, and had sent in
Scott to do the actual fighting. As a result, a bitter feud quickly
developed between the two men.

While there was nothing personal about it, General Clinch
was also unhappy about Scott's assignment. He considered it a
reflection on his conduct of the Battle of the Withlacoochee,
which it undoubtedly was. Within three months Clinch had submitted his resignation, and he thereafter retired to his plantation
in Georgia.

In spite of disgruntled generals, Scott did have the satisfaction of receiving the support of the majority of his countrymen.
With the institution of slavery threatened, the South was solidly
behind the War; the West fervently held to the belief that
Indians anywhere should be taught a lesson; and the chauvinis-
tically inclined Middle Atlantic states were determined that
Dade's Massacre, the murder of Thompson, and the Withlacoochee Battle should be avenged. New England held back until
she could see how the conflict affected her commercial inter-
ests. Only among a very small minority—the Philadelphia
Quakers—was there any mention that the Indians might have
rights or that it might be evil to fight to preserve slavery.

All over the South, companies of volunteers were organized,
often in resplendent uniforms, with plans to leave for the war
zone. In the romantic prose of the period, they were acclaimed
in the newspapers as heroes willing to lay down their lives for
their country and to avenge the horror of Dade's Massacre. A
Charleston officer wrote of the volunteers, "Never did Rome or
Greece in days of yore—nor France or England in modern times
—pour forth a nobler soldiery than the volunteers from
Georgia, Alabama, Louisiana, and South Carolina." Officers
from units of militia from as far away as Pennsylvania, New
Jersey, and New York, including the breastplated and hel-
meted First City Troop of Philadelphia, offered the services of
their units to the War Department. Civilians also patriotically

rallied to the cause. Women's sewing circles stitched flags and uniforms for the departing heroes, and banks in the South agreed to advance funds for the troops should Congressional appropriations be dilatory (not an insignificant gesture, considering the notorious reputation of the Federal Government for tardiness of payment). In Louisiana the Legislature advanced $85,000 to equip its departing militiamen.

The selection of Scott, the hero of 1812 and the victor of the Black Hawk War, to command the troops was greeted enthusiastically. Even the Whig newspapers, while not failing to mention the Administration's blunders in Florida, commended the President's choice of commander. They neglected to mention that Scott was a Whig.

Scott immediately left Washington for Florida. It took him a month to arrive at his headquarters at Picolata on the St. Johns. On his way south he began issuing orders and expected to find, awaiting his arrival in Florida, 3,700 citizen-soldiers armed with rifles, as well as 1,300 Regulars. He also directed that 320,000 rations were to be sent to Picolata, and 250,000 to Tampa Bay. Scott was disappointed on both counts. On reaching Picolata, he found only about a thousand militiamen on the St. Johns River, and the volunteers from Alabama didn't begin to arrive at Fort Brooke until March. The supplies for Tampa Bay were almost on schedule, but the seventy tons designated for the St. Johns headquarters, carried in slow ox-drawn wagons over rough and often almost impassable roads, didn't arrive until late in March.

Scott, however, used his time planning the campaign and holding reviews, which the citizen-soldiers thoroughly detested. He had decided upon the standard three-prong pincer movement that the old army always seemed to favor. Although the movement was highly efficient when everything operated like clockwork and the Indians fought like white men, unfortunately this rarely if ever occurred.

The general concluded that most of the Seminole were in their stronghold in the cove of the Withlacoochee. Accordingly, a column of troops commanded by General Clinch (who had not yet resigned) would leave Fort Drane and head south toward the hostile stronghold. Under Colonel William Lindsay, a force from Tampa Bay would strike northeast. An army led by General Eustis, from Volusia, would cross the peninsula to the cove. It was all very simple and planned according to the book. The Indians, caught in a great pincer move, would be either decisively defeated or, at the least, driven in small bands to the north, where they could be picked off piecemeal. The War would be over. Actually, during the campaign, little happened according to plan.

Back in New Orleans, General Gaines, Commander of the West, did not learn of the Dade Massacre or the Battle of the Withlacoochee until January 15. As West Florida was within the area of his command, he believed that this might be his long-awaited opportunity to command a combat army in the field.

Edmund Pendleton Gaines, a Virginian, had a craggy face with deeply etched lines that gave him the appearance of a Roman tribune. An aristocrat, he generally took good care of his men and was well liked in return. Blunt to a fault, he took "nothing from nobody," not even the President of the United States. Like Scott, he had been one of the few commanders who had distinguished themselves in the War of 1812. Remaining in the army after that war, he had continued in a top position of command.

Without orders from Washington, Gaines left New Orleans on February 4, 1836, with the army he had gathered together. Two days later it was a bitter and fiery general who received a delayed War Department letter advising him that Scott had been given the Florida command.

In the message from Washington there were no instructions as to what Gaines should do, so he continued on to Fort Brooke.

General Edmund Pendleton Gaines

Actually, he was supposed to take command of the troops on the northern border of Texas. He learned of his orders when his armada arrived in Tampa Bay on February 9.

Gaines was now in a quandary. Clinch at Fort Drane might be in dire trouble, needing help. Gaines' every inclination was to lead the troops at Brooke north for the relief of Clinch. A Colonel Persifor F. Smith of the Louisiana Volunteers easily convinced the general where his duty lay. Smith told the general that if he left for the West the militiamen would return to New Orleans.

Gaines moved out on the 13th. Besides the possible need of support for Clinch and his men was the equally compelling necessity for speed. The supplies due at Fort Brooke had not yet arrived, and the general understood there were ample supplies for his troops at Fort King.

Gaines, with a six-pounder and about 1,000 men, followed the old military road north. At the site of the Dade disaster, they found the badly disintegrated bodies of the fallen. Officers and troopers alike were given burial.

General Gaines and his troops arrived at Fort King on February 22, only to find his information had been wrong. There were no supplies. There was nothing to do but dispatch a train of packhorses to Fort Drane to borrow supplies from Clinch. Unfortunately, Clinch could spare but 12,000 rations, and Gaines was forced to set out on a return to Fort Brooke.

This time Gaines decided to follow the path that Clinch had blazed on his way to the Battle of Withlacoochee. The hope that he could meet the Indians and strike a decisive blow before Scott's campaign could get underway was unquestionably in his mind. Gaines left Fort King on February 26 and reached the Withlacoochee the next day. There he camped, sending his scouts out to find a better crossing. They found the ford that Clinch had not known existed. Moving his army to the ford, Gaines made plans to cross. Lieutenant James F. Izard, who was to lead the first contingent, had just stepped into the river when hostiles opened fire. The young lieutenant fell, mortally wounded by a bullet through the head. The engagement that ensued with the Indians across the river lasted from nine o'clock in the morning until four in the afternoon, when the Indians broke off the action. There had been a number of soldiers wounded. That evening the general directed his men to erect a log breastwork enclosing an area of about 250 yards square. He named it Camp Izard in honor of the dying lieutenant. He also dispatched a message to Clinch to come at once before the Indians dispersed.

At dawn bullets began thudding against the logs of the breastwork. Gaines was surrounded. A soldier was killed, and there were now thirty-two wounded. Furthermore, while they had plenty of ammunition, the 12,000 rations Clinch had given them were almost gone. That evening a scout was able to get through the Seminole lines with a second letter for Clinch. In it, Gaines insisted that the commander at Fort Drane come immediately and strike the Indians from the rear. Gaines did not admit that he was surrounded, but Clinch evidently read between the lines or learned of the true situation from the scout who had carried the message.

Days passed, and there was still no word from Clinch. The horses and mules were slaughtered, and the men doled out a meager ration. The situation was becoming desperate. Gaines' command had now been besieged for eight days, and there had been five men killed and forty-six wounded. If Clinch did not arrive soon, Gaines and his men would have to fight their way out of the pocket.

Clinch's failure to move, however, had not been voluntary. General Scott had been furious when he learned that Gaines not only was in Florida but had had the impudence to lead an army within Scott's zone of command. It would spoil all his carefully laid plans. Scott was not a man given to profanity—his oaths nevertheless fairly blistered the canvas of his tent; not a petty man, he acted petulantly. He issued an order to Clinch that he was not to go to Gaines' relief.

Scott, however, was soon over his anger and sent a rescinding order, but by the time it arrived at Fort Drane, Clinch's humanitarian instincts had gotten the better of him, and he had already left for the Withlacoochee. He had already determined to resign from the army, and Scott could "do his damnedest."

On the evening of the day Clinch left Fort Drane, March 5, a bizarre incident occurred at Camp Izard. From the Seminole lines came a voice with a Negro accent, which over the years has been identified as that of either Abraham or John Caesar, calling out asking for a parley the next day. The men and officers, particularly General Gaines, were puzzled, but he had nothing to lose and therefore agreed to the talk.

There was of course a logical explanation for the Indians' conduct. Abraham was one of the few among the Seminole with any understanding of the power of the United States. He knew that the Indians and their Negro allies could not win a prolonged war and that attrition alone would ultimately bring about the defeat of the Seminole. They had won two military victories, and a third was now in prospect. Miles of plantations had been destroyed, and the settlers had been driven from Central and South Florida. Now was the time to negotiate. Perhaps they could win terms that would allow them to remain in Florida.

Together with John Caesar, Abraham had persuaded the Chiefs to follow his suggested course of action. Micanopy, who longed for the easy days of peace, had been easy to swing over. The arguments with Jumper and Alligator had taken longer, but they finally consented to the talks. Even the young firebrand Osceola had admitted the logic of the proposed step and reluctantly fallen into line.

The parley was held the next morning in the open area between the stockade and the Seminole lines. The delegation, consisting of Jumper, Alligator, Osceola and Abraham, approached under a white flag. Representing General Gaines were majors Hitchcock and Barrow, Doctor Harrell, Captain Marks, and the interpreter Hagan. The Indians told the whites that they were tired of fighting, that they would lift the siege and retire south of the Withlacoochee if the general would guarantee that in spite of the treaties they could remain in Florida. There was some further talk. Osceola's only remark during the powwow referred to Dade's Massacre and the murder of Wiley Thompson—"I am satisfied."

Gaines, with the responsibility for almost 1,000 starving men, some of whom were wounded, must have been sorely tempted to agree to the Indians' terms. He was, however, an honorable man, and he sent back word to the afternoon session that he was without authority to make such an agreement, but would present it to the proper officials. The conference had not gone much beyond this point when it came to a sudden end. Clinch's approaching troops, unaware that a parley was in session and seeing the Indians before the breastwork, let loose a volley. The Seminole fled. The first attempt at a negotiated peace ended as a disaster.

With Fort Izard now relieved, its emaciated defenders were fed and the wounded given care. Before returning to Fort Drane, Gaines turned over his command to General Clinch. On March 13 the general started his trip to the West, but before leaving he was forced to spend a day with Scott at Fort Clinch. As *Niles Register* was later to report, the two generals ". . . showed as much courtesy to each other as any two can, who take no notice of each other."

General Scott again returned to his elaborate plans for a victorious termination of the Seminole War. From Fort Drane, on March 14, he ordered Colonel Lindsay, who commanded what the general called the Center Wing at Tampa Bay, and Eustis, commanding the Left Wing at Volusia, to move to their line of departure by March 25. Clinch would leave Fort Drane one day later, with Scott and the Right Wing. Scott now envisioned that the Right Wing would drive the Seminole out of the cove of the Withlacoochee into the arms of the two other forces, poised at Chocachatti (Lindsay's Center Wing) and Peliklakaha (Eustis' Left Wing).

For the three commanders, as their columns moved over the often unmapped rough sand roads, nothing seemed to take place on schedule. Clinch's movement south was again slow, and he did not arrive at the site of Fort Izard until three days after leaving Drane. There he paused to rest his weary men. Mahon notes that, to cheer his tired men, Clinch "ordered the band to play during the evening meal." This of course brought on Indian fire, and that particular supper became an unpleasant memory.[4]

This time Clinch was better prepared for the river crossing. Two flatboats had been built at Fort Drane, fitted on wheels, and dragged the thirty miles to the Withlacoochee. The crossing was made without opposition until the last detachment was afloat. Then fire was received from the north bank and from an island in midstream. The Indians were apparently not in force and were easily driven off. Although there was a skirmish on March 29, when two soldiers were killed and thirteen wounded, it soon became obvious that there was no concentration of Seminole in the cove of the Withlacoochee. The Indians had simply moved away from Scott's pincers.

Though a cannon had been fired by each of the columns at a designated time of day to indicate their position, Scott had not maintained contact with his other two wings, so there was nothing to do but continue on to Fort Brooke, which the Right Wing reached on April 5. There Scott found that Lindsay's force had arrived the previous day.

Colonel Lindsay's report to General Scott was not a happy one. The lack of discipline among the Alabama troops had on

1837 Lithogra

y James & Gray

occasion verged on mutiny. The colonel, it was said, could not visit the volunteers' camp unless guarded by a detachment of marines. Furthermore, the men, in their dislike of Lindsay, seemed to be aided and abetted by the regiment's second in command, Lieutenant Colonel Crabbe. The militiamen complained that Lindsay refused to allow the sutler to sell them whiskey, had restricted them to four rounds of ammunition apiece as punishment for firing at cattle, and had protected some friendly Seminole Indian scouts who they said had wounded one of their comrades. Nor were the Alabamians Lindsay's only personnel problem. Major Leigh Read and his Florida Militia were equally contentious and undisciplined.

Before Lindsay had received Scott's orders to move to his line of departure by March 25, the colonel had employed his troops in building a blockhouse, which he christened Fort Alabama, where the old military road to Fort King crossed the Hillsborough River. He left a small contingent there when he started to march to Chocachatti on March 21. The move took a week, for the column was constantly harassed by small hit-and-run detachments of Indians and Negroes. On March 26 his advance was held up when his troops received fire from the direction of a dense hammock. It was necessary to train his cannon on the hostiles and to order a fixed-bayonet charge before the enemy could be dislodged. There were four casualties, including two killed. At Chocachatti he had tried without success to make contact with Scott, and after three days, with his supplies low, he started the return south. He found Fort Alabama under siege but drove off the Indian and Negro attackers. He reached Fort Brooke on April 4.

A few days later, General Eustis also arrived unexpectedly at Fort Brooke with the Left Wing, and his report was equally depressing. A short, thin-lipped, cool, and aloof Virginian who had entered the army in 1808, Eustis was a strict disciplinarian who played no favorites. He was recognized as an able officer

116

even by the enlisted men. Although he generally wore civilian attire and seldom even carried a sword, he also found it almost impossible to secure prompt obedience from the militia. He might have reported, but didn't, that when the body of an Indian Chief thought to be Yuchi Billy, killed by the militiamen, was brought into camp, it had been scalped, mutilated and trussed on a framework "like a dead wolf."

Against enemy opposition, it had taken Eustis four days to cross the St. Johns River at Volusia. His advance, two companies of the South Carolina Volunteers, lost three men and suffered six wounded before a beachhead could be established. His little army of about a thousand men had at one time taken two days to cover seven miles over the trackless wilderness. It had been necessary to build a bridge over the Oklawaha River, and at Okihumpy, near the town of Micanopy, there had been a heavy battle with the Seminole. Five days later he arrived at his objective, the Negro village of Peliklakaha, the one-time home of Abraham. He found it abandoned, and after burning it, he set his course south for Fort Brooke and the needed supplies.

Winfield Scott was above all an honest man, and his report on the campaign to the War Department was probably the only totally candid one that Washington received during the entire Seminole War. He admitted that fewer than sixty Indians had been killed in the operation; that the convergence of the three wings at Fort Brooke had not been planned, but was the result of faulty logistics; that disease and low morale were rampant among the troops; that the horses had broken down from hard usage; and that the Indians, now in small detachments, were hard to locate. In short, the entire campaign had been a fiasco.

Hoping to salvage *something*, Scott next turned to using the volunteers before their short enlistments expired. Colonel Persifor Smith, with his Louisiana regiment and a naval contingent, was sent by boat to rout some Indians said to be along the south bank of Pease Creek. At the same time, Colonel Goodwyn, with the mounted South Carolina Volunteers, was to scout the north bank of the creek. Clinch, with the Right Wing, and Lindsay, with the Center, were to cover the country drained by the Withlacoochee. They found no Indian concentrations but were continually harassed and drawn into skirmishes with small detachments of hostiles.

On April 4 Doctor John McLemore, now Major McLemore, left a small detachment of fifty of his Florida Militia at a point on the Withlacoochee River twelve miles from its mouth. No one has ever figured out why the men were there, but, under the command of Captain M. K. Holloman, they constructed a twelve-foot-high blockhouse, which was finished on April 10. No enemy was seen until dawn of the 12th, when the hostiles opened up a heavy fire. Thereafter until May 30 the men in the beleaguered fort were given no rest, night or day, by the investing Indians and Negroes.

On April 24 blazing arrows set the blockhouse on fire, but although the roof was destroyed, the building itself remained. The only water supply was a small hole near but outside the stockade, which only filled when the river was at high tide and from which water was drawn in a two-quart tin bucket to which a string was attached. Captain Holloman was killed on May 3 in the course of an effort to increase their water supply by extending the blockhouse to the river, and Lieutenant L. B. Walker took command of the post.

The garrison had been reduced to a starvation diet of a few kernels of corn a day when Sergeant John M. Leek and privates John Rogers and John Riley agreed to make an attempt to reach the outside world for help. On a dark night they set out on the Withlacoochee River in a patched canoe. The Indians fired at the men, but they successfully reached the Gulf of Mexico.

Scott, who didn't even know of the existence of the blockhouse when he received word of the state of its defenders, sent orders to Clinch directing him to go to its relief. After a staff meeting, Clinch came to the conclusion that he did not have sufficient troops to carry out the mission and ignored his orders. There was a month's delay before a force of volunteers under Lindsay's nemesis, Colonel Leigh Read, lifted the siege. The rescued men later charged Scott with having forgotten them.

The Withlacoochee blockhouse siege was not the only one in which the Indians participated during this period. Before Clinch returned, the Seminole attempted to take Fort Drane. They were driven off, but did capture a herd of horses grazing outside the post.

Starting on April 14, Fort Alabama was under almost constant attack, and in late April Colonel Lindsay decided to abandon it, sending Colonel William Chisolm with about 600 troops, mostly Alabama Volunteers, to relieve the garrison and deactivate the fort. On April 27 Chisolm ran smack into an ambush. By that time the citizen-soldiers had acquired some discipline, and they rallied and drove the Indians off. However, five men were killed, and twenty-four wounded.

Colonel Chisolm left Fort Alabama standing, but he had set up a trap—two strings from the door of the blockhouse to the trigger of a musket buried in a barrel of gunpowder. The troops had not gone far from the post when a tremendous explosion was heard. Fort Alabama no longer existed.

Meanwhile, the troops that Scott had dispatched from Fort Brooke had returned to their respective bases, and the volunteers had been discharged and sent home. Like the first phase of the campaign, the second phase had been a complete failure. The troops had taken part in small engagements with the hostiles, had suffered casualties, and unquestionably had killed some Indians, but they had found no concentrations of Seminole.

Tactically, the generalship of the Indians had been superb. In the early days of the War, when the white forces in Florida had been small, they had met the troops squarely and on an equal basis. When Scott arrived and volunteers poured into the

1837 Lithograp

y James & Gray

territory, they broke into small bands and, using guerrilla tactics, harassed the enemy. Scott had allowed himself to be misled by Clinch's Battle of the Withlacoochee into believing that the Seminole could be made to fight like white men. He had been wrong.

Almost daily, articles appeared in the newspapers condemning Scott's conduct of the War. Complaints streamed north from the Territory to the War Department, and Scott's rival Gaines let off a number of vitriolic blasts. Scott himself did not help his cause. With his penchant for sounding off, he wrote Washington on April 30 that 3,000 soldiers, "good troops (not Volunteers)," would be necessary to end the War. His order of May 17, Number 48, deplored the lack of courage of the Floridians, ". . . who saw . . . an Indian in every bush." In St. Augustine and Pensacola, Scott was burned in effigy, and writers referred to him as presumptuous and ignorant.

Whatever it may have thought of his conduct of the War, Washington knew that General Scott's usefulness in Florida had ended. The Creek had gone on the warpath again, and the War Department informed Scott under date of April 15 that he would leave the Territory and take over the troops in Alabama as soon as possible.

On April 25 General Clinch resigned from the army and left for his plantation in Georgia. There Secretary Cass offered him the Florida command. The general was adamant in his decision to leave the army, however, and declined the assignment. His resignation was ultimately accepted.

The War in Florida was not yet over for Scott. In November 1836 a Court of Inquiry convened at Frederick, Maryland, to consider the charges and countercharges of misconduct that Scott and Gaines had made. Scott accused Gaines of having ruined the plans for the campaign by his move into Florida. Gaines bitterly replied that his actions had been necessary, for he had known that Scott would not promptly react to the Indian depredations. Of Scott's order to Clinch not to help him, Gaines said that Scott was " . . the second United States General Officer who has ever dared to assist the enemy. . . . The first great offender was Major General Benedict Arnold; the second as your finding must show, is Major General Winfield Scott."

Scott in turn told the court that he was unable to remember a single blunder, "in my recent operations, or a single duty neglected." True to army tradition the court held that, with the exception of Gaines' violent language and his failure to make a sortie from Camp Izard, both officers were blameless.

CHAPTER XII

The Politician

I wish the Indians would murder every man
in Florida, that the women would get new
husbands and breed children equal when they
grow up to defend their Territory.

ANDREW JACKSON, 1836

In February 1836, the President sent to the Senate for approval
the nomination of Richard K. Call to succeed John Eaton as
Governor of Florida. Eaton was to become Minister to Spain.
Call had long coveted the governorship, but he burned even
more for martial glory—he wanted command of all troops in
the Territory. He was fated to achieve both ambitions.

The Senate gave its consent to the appointment on March
16, shortly after the death of Call's wife. As if trying to forget
his deep loss, he set to work with a vigor the office had not
known since the early years of Eaton.

Before his appointment, Call had written Jackson: "I would
be highly gratified to command the army, and believe I could
soon bring the war to a close." After assuming the governorship,
his letters continued; he wrote the President that with 2,500
men he could conduct a summer campaign (then considered im-

possible in the Florida heat) that would destroy the Indians' crops and end the War. One of his letters sent northward read: "Nothing have I so much desired as to have the direction of the Florida War. . . . The sooner I am placed in command, the sooner shall I be prepared for the field."[1]

Call's pleas had their effect. On May 25, 1836, Secretary of War Cass wrote the governor:

> Should General Scott . . . have left the Territory . . . and should General Clinch not continue in office you are then authorized to assume command of the Regular Forces and militia serving in Florida, and to employ the same in the best manner for the defense of the country, and the speedy subjugation of the Indians.

The governor was overjoyed and went to work with a will. There were only 1,000 Regulars in Florida, hardly enough to conduct the campaign Call contemplated. Pleas went out to Tennessee, South Carolina, and several other Southern states to send volunteers for service in Florida.

Back in Washington, "Andy" Jackson, remembering the impetuosity of his old friend, seemed to have come up with second thoughts—or at least limiting conditions. The day after Secretary Cass' letter to Call, a second message was dispatched south. It read: "If General Jesup in the course of the campaign shall move into Florida, and General Scott shall be absent, he will of course be entitled to, and will assume command."

The selection of a commander for the troops in Florida was not the only subject that was occupying the attention of Washington. In March and April, Congress had passed a bill giving volunteers the same pay and allowance as Regulars and had appropriated $1,500,000 for the conduct of the Seminole War. Now they increased the size of the Regular establishment by adding a second regiment of dragoons. The periods of enlistment for volunteers were extended to six months and a year, rather than the previous enlistment term of three months.

The Jacksonian Democrats saw an opportunity to again bring up one of their favorite subjects, the abolition of West Point, pointing out that its graduates were not being taught to fight Indians successfully. When that argument failed, they proposed that two-thirds of the officers in the new regiment be non-Academy, but that proposal was also defeated.

General Scott did not leave Florida until mid-June, but Call spent the time planning his future operations. Still believing that the Indians and their Negro allies were concentrated in the cove of the Withlacoochee, he advised Jackson by letter that he would use the river as his line of supply, thus obviating the cumbersome wagon trains that delayed the movement of troops. Creating a diversion with mounted volunteers, he planned to move his infantry and supplies up the Withlacoochee at night in fortified boats, thereafter falling upon and defeating the Seminole with ease.

It was all very simple, and Jackson was impressed. He wrote on the back of the letter that "it will redeem us from that disgrace that now hangs over us." Call set about putting his plans into operation.

While the whites were getting their house in order, the enemy was not idle. They kept up a continuous attack on the wagon trains that left Volusia for Fort King—that post's only source of supply.

Logistical difficulties plus its unhealthy climate caused Fort King to be abandoned in late May. The Indians thereafter directed their attention at Fort Drane and Fort Defiance. The latter, a small stockade near the site of Micanopy, was the headquarters of Major Julius F. Heilman, who commanded in the area. Heilman, a New Englander, was the twelfth graduate of West Point. Commissioned in 1806, he was an officer of considerable daring and originality.

The Indians and Negroes gave little rest to Captain Lemuel Gates at Drane. The fort was fired upon almost daily. Also a Yankee and a member of the class of 1806 at the Military Academy, Gates (who was to retire during the Civil War as a brigadier general) grew tired of purely defensive actions. On one occasion he moved a howitzer outside the stockade gates and, unprotected by any works, began lobbing shells into the area where he believed the enemy to be. The barrage was followed by a small force charging the hostiles with fixed bayonets. The Indians took off into the woods, and for a few days the post was left alone.

At Fort Defiance, Major Heilman also became bored with merely defending the post. A group of about 250 Indians and Negroes attacked the fort on June 9. Heilman had only about seventy men fit for duty, but he decided to try a double envelopment of the hostile position, in a nearby hammock. A detachment of dragoons was sent around the Seminole's left flank, a company of Red Legs around the right, while still another group of miscellaneous troops attacked the center. At a given signal, the foot artillery charged the hostile rear while the dragoons galloped toward their objective. To add to the din, Heilman at the same time advanced from the fort with a six-pounder and its crew, firing at the hammock as he went. The Indians and their allies, suffering losses, vanished into the woods. Heilman, who did not have any casualties, won the brevet of lieutenant colonel that day.

Fort Drane, the principal post in the area, became Major Heilman's headquarters when he moved there on June 11. He found the garrison in poor shape. One-third of the troops were down with malaria, and the morale among the remainder was consequently low. A short time after Heilman arrived at Drane he contracted the fever, and he died from it on June 27.

With ninety-nine of his 289 men ill, Captain Charles S. Merchant, who had succeeded Heilman in command at Drane, recommended to Governor Call that the unhealthy post be abandoned. The governor, in spite of his belief in the feasibility of a summer campaign in the semi-tropics in 1836, agreed and directed Merchant to withdraw to Fort Defiance.

Remaining behind with the sick, and with sufficient troops to hold the post, Merchant had Captain William S. Maitland begin the move on July 19, 1836. With a train of twenty-two wagons loaded with supplies and an escort of sixty-two men, twenty-six of whom were mounted, Maitland set off before dawn. They had covered nine of the ten miles separating the two posts when Osceola, with about 200 warriors, opened fire on the long, drawn-out column. The rifle fire was heard at Fort Defiance, and a detachment of thirty-one men was sent to the rescue. The combined forces, in a charge, were able to drive the enemy back to a point where cannons could be employed. The hostiles then withdrew, but Merchant had suffered five killed and six wounded in what has been called the Battle of Welika Pond. There was another minor attack before the post was reached, but it was easily driven off.

At Fort Drane, Merchant next appealed to Call for an escort of 250 men to move the sick to Fort Defiance, but the governor was not able to send any troops until August 7, when the move was made without incident.

Central Florida was now practically inundated by whites, and the Seminole extended the scope of their activities. On July 23 they attacked the lighthouse on the southern end of Key Biscayne. The keeper, John Thompson, and his Negro helper first defended themselves on the ground floor of the lighthouse, but when the stored oil used to fuel the light was ignited, they were forced to climb the ninety feet to the top. Thompson dropped down a keg of powder, hoping that if it did not topple the tower it would drive off his attackers. However, it did little damage, and the hostiles kept up their steady fire. The Negro was killed and Thompson was wounded in both feet before the Indians withdrew. He was rescued the next day by a party from the United States Schooner *Motto*. They had heard the explosion and changed course for Key Biscayne. The old man was brought down from the top of the burned-out lighthouse by a sort of breeches buoy that the ingenious sailors contrived.[2]

On July 28 Second Lieutenant Alfred Herbert, only a year out of the Academy, who was out on a scouting mission in force, surprised a group of Indians and Negroes near the Travers plantation, east of the St. Johns River. Opening fire at forty paces, Herbert's men killed four of the enemy, but the Indians' strength was too much for the whites, who were finally forced to withdraw to their boats.

On August 15 Major Benjamin K. Pierce, a New Hampshire–born veteran of the War of 1812, was sent from St. Augustine with 125 men and a train of twenty-six wagons to deactivate Fort Defiance. He learned that the hostiles had done the obvious and occupied the abandoned Fort Drane. Leaving his wagons at Defiance on August 21, he set out with a cannon and about a hundred men, half of whom were mounted on the wagon horses, for the abandoned post. Galloping into Drane, his force took the Indians by surprise, and they scattered into the woods, eventually taking a position in a hammock, from which they opened fire. Using canister, Pierce tried to dislodge them, but after an hour in which he lost two killed and sixteen wounded, he withdrew. He was awarded a brevet of lieutenant colonel.

Colonel John Warren of the Florida Militia, who had rendered such creditable service in the first Battle of the Withlacoochee, was next to tangle with the Seminole. On September 18, on a reconnaissance in force with a hundred men and a six-pounder, he was attacked by a large force of Indians and Negroes in an area called the San Felasco Hammock. The hostiles

1837 Lithogra

James & Gray

tried to turn his flank but were stopped by a mounted charge and the effective use of the cannon. Thereafter Warren was able to withdraw.

Call planned a campaign using the approximately 1,000 Regulars then in Florida; miscellaneous militia, the most important of which was a contingent of about 1,500 Tennessee Volunteers, whom General Scott had promised to send to Florida; and a newly organized regiment of friendly Creek warriors. The latter were organized and led by a young, swashbuckling extrovert, Colonel John F. Lane.*

The summer during which Call had assured Jackson his campaign would be conducted had come and gone before the Tennessee troops Scott had promised arrived in Tallahassee. They had heard of the fighting in Florida, the long hard marches through wild and unexplored country, the battles which were often fought waist-deep in swamp water, and were not happy to be there. They were also unenthusiastic about serving under the command of a governor who held no military rank. Nevertheless, on September 18 they arrived in the Territorial capital.

Although formulated without a basic knowledge of logistics, Call's plans called for the establishment of four main supply points, all of which were to be located on navigable waters, at Volusia, at Tampa, at Suwannee Old Town, and at a spot twenty miles up the Withlacoochee River. The latter two had not been established when the Tennesseans arrived in Florida. The gov-

---

* Although a West Pointer, Lane was a product of the frontier, having been born in Kentucky and raised in Indiana. An ardent admirer of General Jackson, he had come to the latter's attention on a Washington street when he flogged Representative John Ewing of Indiana, a critic of the President. He was the inventor of a pontoon bridge that was successfully and widely used during and after the War in Florida. He was only eight years out of the Academy and only a captain in the Second Dragoons when promoted to colonel and given the Creek Regiment assignment.

ernor accordingly ordered Colonel Leigh Read, the rescuer of
the defenders of the Withlacoochee blockhouse, to proceed by
the steamship *Izard* with a large force of Florida Militia and a
contingent of Regulars to the designated spot on the Withlacoochee and there set up the necessary depot. The *Izard*, operated by naval officers, was to tow up the river two specially built
flatboats manned by sailors.

On September 29, Call left the Suwannee River with the
main body of his troops and ten days' rations on pack mules and
headed for Fort Drane. On the way he surprised and killed a
small party of Indians. When he arrived at the fort on October
1 he found it abandoned and burned. He did, however, observe
a large column of smoke in the distance. The next day a detachment of 200 men was sent on a reconnaissance and discovered a
burned Indian village of about 150 huts. It appeared to have
been precipitately abandoned the previous day. Call believed the
encampment to have been inhabited by Mikasukies led by Osceola. Another report had it that at the time Call's troops arrived
in the vicinity of Fort Drane, Osceola was down with fever in
the nearby village.

On the 8th, Call's troops were joined at Fort Drane by
Major Pierce, with additional supplies and 200 Regulars. The
next day the combined force started the march south toward the
cove of the Withlacoochee. On the 12th they unexpectedly
came on a group of about fifty warriors, fourteen of whom they
killed. They arrived at the river opposite the cove on the 14th.
Unfortunately, Call's quartermaster had failed to bring along
axes with which to construct rafts, and an attempt was made to
cross by swimming the horses. The first contingent was met with
withering fire from the west bank, and the attempt finally had to
be abandoned. Call next sent a contingent of Tennessee troops
downstream to discover a ford, but with the river swollen by
rains they were unable to find a suitable crossing spot.

After a staff conference Call determined that he would keep

133

his troops on the east bank of the river, proceeding northward until his force had reached the supply depot that Colonel Read had supposedly established. After three days of such wandering, with rations practically gone and the horses dying for lack of forage, Call turned northward and, without one major engagement, retraced his steps to Fort Drane. It was a disaffected, hungry, and grumbling army that arrived at the burned-out post on October 17.

Call had not found Colonel Read's supply depot, for it had not then existed. The *Izard* had entered the river, but shortly thereafter had grounded and broken up, and it was not until October 22 that Read's men, after heroic exertions, literally carrying the supplies through the jungle on their backs, established the post at the point Call had designated.

At Fort Drane the governor was joined by Colonel Lane and his regiment of 750 friendly Creek. They had arrived at Fort Brooke late in September and immediately started the move north. Following a small engagement with the Seminole, they crossed the Withlacoochee near the cove and continued their march. Their commander had, however, had enough. Shortly after arrival at Fort Drane, he went to his tent and—for reasons that have yet to emerge—drew his sword and plunged it through his right eye into his brain.

His command was taken over by Lieutenant Colonel Harvey Brown.

Call did not send Jackson a report of his abortive operations, but the story of the campaign, carried by Lieutenant Alexander M. Mitchell, reached the War Department. Jackson, who had always had in his mind a nagging doubt of Call's military abilities, was furious when he learned of the retrograde movement. He was reported to have exclaimed, "With fifty women I could defeat all the Indians who have been ravaging the area west of the Suwannee." He also took action. Acting Secretary of War Benjamin F. Butler was directed to write to Call advising him that the President was disappointed that Call had started his campaign without adequate supplies and had not attacked the Seminole stronghold when they were so near. The governor was advised that he was relieved and should turn over his command to Major General Thomas S. Jesup, who was being ordered to the Territory. Lieutenant Mitchell had reported that Governor Call was not well, so Secretary Butler diplomatically gave poor health as the reason for Call's relief. The letter, dated November 4, did not reach Call for over a month.

On November 10, ignorant of the developments in Washington, Call once more set out from Drane for the cove of the Withlacoochee. His army of Florida Militia, Tennessee Volunteers, the friendly Creek, and a contingent of Regulars, probably close to 2,500 men, reached the river on November 13. Dividing his army so that he might execute a pincer movement in the cove, his two forces crossed the river without opposition. This time there were plenty of axes, and the only casualties were four men who fell off the rafts with full packs and were drowned. When the pincers came together, Call found the Indian stronghold, three large Indian villages, but all had been abandoned.

Determined to find the dispersed Seminole, Call next decided on a search-and-destroy operation. Sending Colonel Pierce with the Creek Regiment and a miscellaneous assortment of Florida Militia and Regulars southward, he took the rest of the force back across the river to search that side. The two forces were supposed to converge at the site of Dade's battlefield. Call's troops were to see more action than Pierce's.

The Tennessee Volunteers stumbled on a large Indian encampment on November 17. After a charge by the white troops, the Indians broke. In the pursuit that followed, the volunteers, often waist-deep in water, killed twenty of the red men and captured their horses and baggage. The whites suffered only one dead and ten wounded.

Another engagement took place the next day, after the

scouts reported a concentration of warriors in a hammock facing an open field. Call ordered detachments to attack the enemy flank. When it appeared that the attackers might be enveloped, Call directed that they should dismount and execute a direct charge at the hostile flanks, on a line at a right angle to his main troops. The Indians and Negroes broke, losing twenty-five killed to only three whites dead and twelve wounded.

Call next recrossed the river and moved to his rendezvous point, arriving there on November 21, a day before Pierce. With intelligence that the hostiles were concentrated in the nearby Wahoo Swamp, along the east bank of the Withlacoo-chee, Call joined the two forces and moved his troops north-ward.

It was not long before the elusive foe were found in a heavy wood bordering on an open field. With the Creek allies on the left, the Florida Militia and the Regulars in the center, and the Tennesseans on the right, the troops charged across the open field, and the enemy soon gave way.

Continuing in pursuit for over a mile and a half of swamp mud and water, Call's men came to a ten-yard-wide cedar stream. No one knew its depth, and when Major David Moniac, a Creek and the first Indian to graduate from West Point, waded in to find out, he was dropped by a Seminole bullet. The water was only three feet deep. Call decided not to make a crossing. Instead he withdrew and marched his troops the sixty miles back across the peninsula to Volusia. Later he claimed that his rations were low and it was necessary to get to a supply point. Evidently he had forgotten that the depot he had directed Colonel Leigh Read to establish on the Withlacoochee was nearby. He did not realize that he had been on the threshold of a great victory. Beyond the rivulet lay a Seminole village where over 600 Indians and Negro warriors and their women and chil-dren had lived undisturbed since the start of the War. Once they were back at Volusia, Captain Henry Hollingsworth wrote bitterly in his diary, "That is Callism."

The governor had not been at Volusia long when the mail caught up with him, and he received Acting Secretary Butler's month-old letter relieving him of his command. It was gall and wormwood to the lawyer-politician who had dreamed of martial glory. And now the President, his friend of years, had betrayed him on the word of a lieutenant. On December 2 Call dispatched a bitter letter to Jackson defending his campaign. It was a futile and final gesture. On December 9 he turned over his command to General Jesup and reluctantly turned his steps toward the Territorial capital to resume his civil duties.

CHAPTER XIII

The Quartermaster

I will not make Negro-catchers of the army.

THOMAS S. JESUP, 1837

Thomas Sidney Jesup prided himself above all things on being a soldier and not a politician. He was certainly not a glory seeker, particularly at the expense of other men's lives. Rather he seemed to seek anonymity, an attribute of all good quartermasters. His firm belief that "the end justifies the means" was to cloud his record in Florida for the rest of his life and to make him a favorite whipping boy of historians.

Born in Virginia in 1788, he later moved with his family to Ohio, from where in 1808 he received, directly from civil life, a commission as a second lieutenant. His subsequent rise during the War of 1812 was rapid. Cited for bravery in the battles of Chippewa and Lund's Lane, by war's end he held the brevet of colonel. In 1818, at the age of thirty, he was named a brigadier and Quartermaster General of the Army. He remained in that capacity for the rest of his life, even while serv-

General Thomas S. Jesup

ing in combat against the Creek in Georgia and Alabama and against the Seminole in Florida. He was to die in 1860. As Mahon notes: "No other United States officer has ever held a staff position for so long [over forty-two years]."[1]

Jesup was in his late forties when he took over from Call. Of medium height, with sparse white hair, clear piercing eyes, and a firm jaw, he gave no outward indication of the duplicity with which he would later be charged. Although he was a strict disciplinarian, he was not a martinet and not addicted to the flamboyance of a Scott.

The general's assumption of command of the War in Florida did not come under as auspicious circumstances as had greeted Clinch, Scott, or even Call. There were indications that the War was becoming unpopular throughout the nation. Word had come back of the horrible conditions under which the troops lived and fought in Florida. Returning soldiers told of marches through swamps with mud and water up to their waists, sword palmettos that tore the clothing and skin, and a disease-casualty rate that was far higher than that from combat. The Tennessee diarist Hollingsworth wrote on the conditions of the troops in the sub-tropics: "A life of dirt and toil, privations and vexations, and the poorest pay in the world, $6 per month."[2] And Doctor Jacob Rhett Motte would later add:

> After all Florida is certainly the poorest country that ever two people quarreled for. The climate in the first place is objection-able; for even in winter, while persons further north were freez-ing, we were melted with heat. In the next place, the larger portion of Florida is a poor, sandy country in the north; and in the southern portions all wet prairies and swamp; healthy in winter but sickly in summer; and in the south even the Indians said they could not live a month without suffering, and in sum-mer not at all. It is in fact a most hideous region to live in. . . . Then why not in the name of common sense let the Indians keep it?[3]

140

The War had lost its early glamour and volunteers became hard to come by. Even those who were bored with their home-life and wanted to shirk their family responsibilities in the name of patriotism had second thoughts. No additional troops arrived from the District of Columbia, and even in Georgia, Louisiana and Tennessee, there was a paucity of recruits.

Nor were the Regulars any happier with service in Florida than the volunteers. The sympathy of both officers and enlisted men was with the Indians, and they condemned the conflict as "a dirty little war of aggression." During 1836 a total of 103 company-grade army officers resigned, mostly to avoid service in Florida. Those of the regular service were willing to concede the treachery of the Seminole and to admit the cruelties that the hostiles had committed on the settlers, but were almost unanimous in insisting that the whites should not have been there in the first place.

Assistant Surgeon Motte, who with pride, almost glee, had left his home in Charleston, South Carolina, in early June 1836 to fight for his country, summed up the feeling of many officers and men when he later wrote of the Florida settlers who had congregated for protection in the little town of Newnansville:

> . . . They were mostly small farmers who had emigrated from different states and settled in Alachua County (Florida) to plant corn, hoe potatoes, and beget ugly little white-headed responsibilities which occupations they pursued with praiseworthy industry and perseverance in the piping times of peace; but imagining it much easier to be fed by Uncle Sam, they provoked the Indians by various aggressions to a retaliation, and then complained to their venerable uncle of the mischievous disposition of his red nephews. He immediately issued his mandate to the said curiously colored relations, that as they could not live in brotherly affection with his white nephews and nieces, their health must be in a bad shape, and a change of air would be very beneficial; whereupon he prescribed that west of the Mississippi as being very pure and wholesome. Uncle Sam's red relations not coinciding

with him on the subject of their health, and discovering the authors of their uncle's displeasure, undertook to revenge themselves upon their white cousins who immediately congregated in spots, built pickets or stockades—which they called forts—drew rations —as they designated themselves "suffering inhabitants"—and devoted their attention entirely to the last of their former occupations.

Finding this a very agreeable way of living, they occasionally united together, and riding through the country in strong parties managed to kill a stray Indian or two. This so exasperated the rest of the tribe that they would break out anew and swear they wouldn't cease hostilities so long as a white-skin of them was left. (I state it as a general opinion, not mine.)[4]

There were also signs of a growing disenchantment with the conduct of the War among the nation's civilian population. A speaker in Congress would lament the cost of the War. A newspaper editorial would deplore the inability of the army to bring the conflict to an end. The complaints and criticisms were not confined to the Northeast. At a dinner in St. Augustine, a toast was given to Osceola, "the great untaken and still unconquered red man" who was fighting for his home.[5]

Although there seemed to be an anti-War sentiment throughout the nation, which would increase during his stay in Florida, General Jesup did have one very distinct advantage that had not been entirely accorded his predecessors. The Seminole War had slowly developed into a combined operation of the military services. This was not based on a command structure, but rather on a general feeling that "we are in this thing together, so let's get it over with." Actually there seemed to be less jealousy among the services than existed within each service. On occasions, army officers commanded sailors and marines, naval officers commanded soldiers and marines, and marine officers commanded soldiers and sailors. These arrangements generally worked without a hitch.

There had been growing cooperation among the services from the start of the War. As noted, following Dade's Massacre the United States Revenue Cutter *Washington* was the first ship to arrive at Fort Brooke. She landed men and guns and later took up a position guarding the passage to the river. For almost three years thereafter, a group of revenue cutters, as part of the naval fleet in the Florida waters, were used as pickets patrolling the coast. Because of their lesser draft, they were able to go up the rivers and on occasion actually enter the Everglades.

Commodore Alexander J. Dallas was in Havana in January 1836, when word arrived of the Dade disaster. He immediately set sail for Key West with the *Constellation* and the *St. Louis*. From there, without waiting for orders from Washington, he went into action, sending all the marines he could spare from the squadron "for the relief of Fort Brooke and also . . . a detachment of seamen to look after the Lighthouse on Cape Florida." The Commodore was determined to give the land forces every support possible.

This cooperation continued for the entire War. Not only was a naval squadron kept in Florida waters to patrol the coast, but naval personnel manned small boats and canoes in the swamps, and sailors and soldiers took part in land engagements. In 1838 the navy organized the so-called Mosquito Fleet, composed of patrol craft, revenue cutters, barges, old naval craft, and even canoes. They ranged the coast, rivers, and the Everglades, and saw considerable hard fighting. Shortly after Jesup took command, most of the forts in Florida were garrisoned by seamen.

The force that First Lieutenant Nathaniel S. Waldron, USMC, set out with on January 17, 1836, for the relief of Fort Brooke included the first sizeable detachment of leathernecks to participate in the Seminole War. Thereafter marines were to participate in almost every campaign and major engagement. It was not, however, until shortly after the arrival of General Jesup that the marine corps became an important factor in the

United States Mari

netrating the Everglades, by J. Clymer

War. The Commandant of Corps, Colonel Archibald Henderson, was responsible.

A short, heavy-set, gutsy man, Henderson was a familiar figure in Washington. Always spoiling for a fight, he had gathered together all the leathernecks he could find in the Washington area, amounting to two battalions, and then taken off for Florida. Marine corps legend has it that he gleefully tacked a notice on his office door:

> Gone to fight the Indians.
> Will be back when the war is over.
>
> A. HENDERSON
> COL. COMDT.

On June 2, 1836, the Washington *National Intelligencer* reported that Colonel Henderson had taken south with him thirty-eight officers and 424 enlisted men, more than half of the marine corps of that day. Proceeding by river steamer to Norfolk (the first time a detachment of marines ever traveled by steam engine), by sail to Charleston, South Carolina, and by rail to Hamburg, on the opposite side of the river from Augusta, Georgia, Henderson and his leathernecks then marched to the Creek country south of Columbus, Georgia. Following the Creek campaign, the two battalions of marines were shipped to Tampa Bay in time to join Governor Call's army and participate in the Battle of Wahoo Swamp.

General Jesup arrived at Fort Brooke in early December. Gathering a small force, he marched across the peninsula to relieve Governor Call at Volusia. On the way, at the head of the Oklawaha River, he found a Negro village which he burned after taking forty-one Negro prisoners.

The term of service of Call's Tennessee Volunteers was about to expire, but Jesup was determined to get as much service from them as possible; so, assembling as many troops as available, including the Tennessee Volunteers, he set out from Vo-

146

Brevet Brigadier General Archibald Henderson

lusia and headed for Tampa Bay. On the way he induced the
Tennessee Volunteers to join with the other troops in constructing a new fort at the site of Dade's battleground. After naming
it Fort Armstrong, in honor of Colonel Robert Armstrong, a
New York West Point graduate who had died in 1834, and
leaving a garrison of about 150 men, he sent the Tennessee
Volunteers back to Fort Brooke for their discharge and with the
remainder of his force proceeded to scout the Wahoo Swamp
and the cove of the Withlacoochee. Jesup's immediate command
now consisted of 450 Regulars, 350 marines, 350 Alabama
Volunteers, and the Creek Regiment.

Jesup next dispatched letters asking for twelve-month volunteers to the governors of the southeastern states. The governors in turn found that the filling of their quotas was not easy,
even though in his letter Jesup had described the conflict as a
Negro and not an Indian War.

The building of Fort Armstrong had been a part of Jesup's
evolving plan. He envisioned a chain of forts that would make it
possible to hold the valley of the Withlacoochee. Fort Drane
was reactivated; Fort Clinch was built near the mouth of the
Withlacoochee; Fort Alabama was rebuilt and redesignated
Fort Foster; and thirty miles north of the latter, Fort Dade was
established. All but Armstrong were garrisoned by seamen lent
to Jesup by the cooperative Commodore Dallas.

Determined that most of his time would be spent in the
field, Jesup next gave the command of North Florida to a Virginia Regular and West Point graduate, Brevet Brigadier General Walker K. Armistead. The troops required to defend this
Zone of the Interior were, as far as possible, to be restricted to
seamen and Florida Militia.

Meanwhile, the general and his troops continued to scour
the valley of the Withlacoochee, but without much success.
Some fifty-two Negroes were taken prisoner, and a small party
of hostiles, said to be led by Osceola, were pursued.

In mid-January Jesup's force was joined by four companies of Volunteer Georgia Cavalry that the governor of that state had been able to raise and by the regular Sixth Infantry Regiment. The latter, however, being destined for the West, was only on temporary loan in Florida.

Unlike his predecessors in command, Jesup had reached the conclusion that if the Indians continued to refuse to concentrate their forces and fight like white men, he would have to use their methods of warfare. When intelligence indicated the location of the presence of a band of hostiles, rather than sending out the entire army, he would send a mobile detachment in pursuit. This new policy was to pay immediate dividends.

Jesup left Fort Armstrong on January 22 with his augmented force. The very next day, word came of the presence of a band of Seminole near Lake Apopka. A detachment sent in pursuit surprised the band, killing Chief Osuchee, four warriors, and taking eight prisoners of war, all Negroes.

Next, Marine Colonel Henderson,* whom Jesup had named commander of his Second Brigade, followed the trail to where

---

* Henderson's personal courage that day was to cause him some problems several years later. Following the battle, he was made a Brevet Brigadier General by the army and became the first officer in the marine corps to reach flag rank. At times a brevet carries with it some increase in pay, and Henderson took full advantage of his brevet promotion. In 1845, the bureaucratic Navy Secretary J. Y. Mason decided that the army could not confer a brevet on a marine and demanded that Henderson reimburse the navy for $12,698.33 overpayment of salary. The colonel and/or brevet brigadier general took the matter directly to a fellow Virginian, President James Polk. A special board, headed by the senior United States military officer, General Winfield Scott, was convened. The board unanimously found in favor of Henderson, who kept his pay increase. That, however, was not the end of the matter, for the following year Secretary Mason induced Congress to add a rider to the naval appropriation bill that read, "No payment shall hereafter be made to a colonel, or any other officer of the Marine Corps, by virtue of a commission of brigadier general by brevet." Herne notes that the resulting pay cut was ". . . one of Archibald Henderson's few recorded defeats."[6]

149

the Hatcheelustee Creek drained into Lake Tohopekliga. There, on January 27, a fairly heavy engagement took place. The Seminole camp was overrun, and a hundred ponies, most of the supplies, five Indians, and twenty-three Negroes were captured. Henderson ordered a pursuit of the withdrawing hostiles, which led the army into the Big Cypress Swamp,[7] but the troops were stopped by a twenty-five-yard creek, and most of the enemy were able to get away.

Besides Henderson's Brigade, Jesup had a number of other detachments seeking the Indian bands. Lieutenant Colonel Fanning was following the St. Johns in search of Chief Philip. A detail of dragoons was stationed in the vicinity of Newnansville. Lieutenant Colonel Foster, with a detachment of over 500, was searching the swamps south of the Withlacoochee, and General Hernandez was covering the area east of the St. Johns River with his Florida Militia.

Jesup's system appeared successful. On February 3, under a flag of truce, Abraham, Micanopy, and Jumper came in for a talk. It is doubtful that the Indians would have made this acknowledgment that they were tired of the War had they not been constantly harassed and kept on the move. It was agreed that there would be an armistice until February 18, when the talks would be resumed at Fort Dade. Neither side, however, kept the truce. Jesup's detachments continued to seek the hostiles, and the Indians would of course fight back when discovered.

Then on February 8, near the St. Johns at the head of Lake Monroe, Colonel Fanning and his detachment had a sharp engagement with over 500 Indian and Negro warriors led by Philip and his son Coacoochee, whom the whites called Wildcat. Fanning would have been in dire trouble had not a naval steamer on the lake opened up on the Seminole with both grapeshot and canister.

The very next day Colonel Foster and his troops discovered a large Indian camp on the Crystal River, south of Fort Clinch. He immediately attacked, aided by a detachment of sailors in small boats who rowed toward the sound of the guns. Many Indian supplies were captured and destroyed, but the warriors were again able to withdraw.

At Fort Dade, General Jesup waited for the 18th and the return of the Seminole emissaries. Jesup knew his logistics and, unlike his predecessors, had been able to keep his forces constantly in the field for over two months. But he knew that, while he had harassed the enemy and kept them on the move, he had hardly conquered the Seminole Nation. He also grasped a fundamental fact that Washington consistently either refused or seemed unable to understand—that this was even more a Negro than an Indian War.

The Seminole unquestionably wanted to remain in Florida, but their love of the land was not so great that they would have been unwilling to remove beyond the Mississippi rather than fight the great colossus of the North. However, whenever talk of compromise occurred, their Negro advisors and allies pressed the point that the policy of the United States was not the migration but rather the annihilation of the Seminole people. This argument's element of truth was indeed convincing.

The Negroes were moved by a fear that a western migration could only result, for them, in a return to bondage. Though the Indian might reach the promised western lands, the Negro never would. Before the Negroes left Florida or while they were on their way to Oklahoma, slave catchers would take them, and they would be returned to that state from which they or their parents had fled. Unfortunately, their fears were well founded. There can be little doubt that the settlers in Florida, most of the whites in the Southeast, and a large majority of those governing the nation in Washington would have preferred to see the Seminole Negroes returned to slavery. The Indian Negroes had experienced little contact with those who felt otherwise.

Either because of the breakdown of the truce or because of fear, February 18 came and went without any signs of the Seminole leaders. A few days later several minor Chiefs arrived at Dade, but Jesup refused to meet with them unless Micanopy and Abraham were present. It wasn't until March that Jumper, Holatoochee, and Yaholoochee convinced General Jesup that they represented Micanopy, with authority to act for him.

On March 6, 1837, a treaty or agreement was concluded, and was signed by Micanopy's alleged representatives. It provided, among other things, that the fighting should end immediately, the Seminole agreeing to withdraw south of the Hillsborough River; that on or before April 10 the Indians would present themselves at Fort Brooke for shipment west of the Mississippi; and that while waiting to leave, during the trip, and for one year after arrival in the West, the Seminole were to be fed by the United States government. Probably the most important clause in the agreement provided "the Seminoles and their allies, who come in and emigrate west, shall be secure in their lives and property . . . their Negroes, their *bona fide* property shall accompany them to the West." The War appeared to be over.

Announcement of the peace terms was greeted with a storm of protest in Florida and as far north as Washington. Jesup, the newspapers screamed, was squandering the sacrifice of the brave heroes who gave their lives for their country. As one Floridian blandly put it: "The regaining of our slaves constitutes an object of scarcely less moment than that of the peace of the Country."

General Jesup had entered into the agreement with the Indian Chiefs in good faith. He wanted to end the War, and he knew that unless it was understood that the Negroes were to go west with the Seminole, the conflict would continue. However, the external pressures quickly began to erode the treaty's honorable terms.

On April 5 Jesup issued Order No. 70, forbidding any whites from going south of the Hillsborough River. On the 8th he began insisting that the Indians turn over any fugitive slaves captured or given asylum during the War. Thereafter he was assailed in Congress by both the pro- and the anti-slavery forces. On May 1 he amended Order 70 to allow white owners of land south of Fort Foster to enter the forbidden territory. It was of course impossible to tell slave catchers from owners, and the enforcement of Order 70 practically came to an end.

Although the deadline of April 10 was not met, the Indians seemed to be trying to keep their end of the bargain. By that date, Chief Yaholoochee and his band were at Tampa ready for migration. By the end of May, Micanopy, Abraham, Cloud, Jumper, Alligator, and their followers, altogether about 700, were in a detention camp, awaiting the start of their westward journey. Unfortunately for the success of General Jesup's program, Tampa was also overrun with slave catchers.

On the night of June 2 the Indian encampment on Tampa Bay was surrounded by 200 warriors under the leadership of Osceola and Sam Jones. The Indians fled the encampment. The Seminole War resumed.

Following the failure of his program, Jesup first asked to be relieved. However, by June 22, when the Commanding General of the Army, Alexander Macomb, offered him an opportunity to leave Florida, Jesup had decided that the abuse he had received had been so great that his leaving would seem to be an acknowledgment of defeat. He was not a man "to quit under fire."

The feverish summer months, when it was all but impossible for white troops to carry out an effective campaign in Florida, had started. General Jesup devoted his time to plans for the fall campaign, the ever-recurring problems of logistics, and the administration of his army.

Jesup next endeavored to lure the more moderate Alachua bands away from the more warlike Seminole tribes by intimating that good Indians might perhaps be allowed to remain in Florida. Few Alachua took the bait.

Next the general proposed to President Martin Van Buren's new Secretary of War, Joel Roberts Poinsett,* that the Seminole be allowed to remain in Florida until their land was needed for settlement. Poinsett's reaction was "no"—such a concession would only show weakness on the part of the government.

Jesup's plans for the fall campaign called for an army of about 6,000 men, including 1,600 for garrison duty, 750 for escort of supplies, and 3,700 to be divided into four mobile columns, one of which would move along the St. Johns River, a second that would patrol Mosquito Inlet, a third that would move from Tampa down the Kissimmee River, and a fourth that would go up the Caloosahatchee. Governor Call was to have command of West Florida, Brevet Brigadier General Armistead was to continue in Northeast Florida, and Marine Colonel Henderson would have authority in the combat zone. Poinsett, a South Carolinian who was one of our best Secretaries of War, agreed. Having some knowledge of the Florida climate, he suggested that the campaign not start until November. The secretary also directed that Jesup use citizen-soldiers and that they not all be mounted, as that would bankrupt the government.

General Jesup had hoped against hope that he would not be required to use volunteers. He was annoyed at their lack of enthusiasm for the War, particularly on the part of the Florida Militia, who were defending their own country. However, he was not entirely happy with the Regulars, who also were obviously disinclined to serve against the Seminole. He wrote in August to the Adjutant General: "It may be truly said the spirit

---

* Whose name is immortalized in the flower he later brought back from Mexico.

of the service is gone when officers abandon the high and honorable duties of their profession to become schoolmasters at West Point."

One has the feeling that General Jesup was at his happiest when dealing with questions of logistics. He asked of his temporary replacement in Washington that he be sent efficient quartermaster officers. He requested and received Dearborn wagons, whose wide tires allowed them to be drawn through the sand easily and which, since they were waterproof, could on occasion be used as boats on the many Florida rivers. Requests for tents, haversacks, kettles, canteens, mess kits, rainproof rubber cloth, flat-bottomed boats and proper rations all received the general's personal attention. Colt revolvers, Cochron repeaters and shotguns were all requisitioned and received.*

The fall campaign was off to an auspicious start in early September. On the 4th four Negroes belonging to a Major Heriot inexplicably deserted the Indians and turned themselves in at Fort Payton, a small post consisting of four log houses in a hollow square, situated on a slight elevation near Moultrie Creek. Perhaps these Negroes were more afraid of the white man's army than they were of his slavery. They reported that they had left a large body of Seminole in the vicinity of Mosquito Lagoon, and General Hernandez set out after the Indians with a force consisting of 170 men, including two companies of the Second Dragoons, one company of the Third Artillery, and two companies of Florida Militia. Also with the troops was the assistant surgeon, Jacob Motte. They left Fort Payton on September 7 and that evening were at what had been Bulow's Mill, on the Halifax River, some thirty miles south of St. Augustine, where they camped overnight. The next morning, they met five additional Negroes, who also had left the Indians. Among the

---

* The army, however, true to form, also sent him a number of unrequested mountain howitzers, which were totally useless in Florida.

blacks was John Philip, a Negro slave of Chief Philip, whose wife had tired of the hardships of life with the Seminole and had induced him to desert to the whites. He either agreed or was forced to lead the troops to the Seminole encampment he had left. Pressing on through an almost impassable swamp at the bend of the Tomoka River, at sunset the white soldiers arrived at a point about a half mile from the ruins of Dunlawton Plantation. A reconnaissance team was sent out and reported the nearby presence of the Indian camp. At midnight the Militia, under Lieutenant D. W. Whitehurst, left their horses and took up a position on three sides of the Seminole camp. The remainder of the troops, mounted, were drawn up in a line along the open fourth side of the red men's position.

Assistant Surgeon Motte tells in his journal of the subsequent engagements:

. . . Just as the day began to dawn, the signal for a charge was given; on we rushed; every man trying to be the first in at the death. We soon found ourselves in the presence of royalty, for there stood King Philip the principal chief on the St. John's River naked as he was born.

We captured the whole party except Philip's youngest son, a lad of eighteen years who escaped into the neighboring hammock by his uncommon agility. Among the prisoners taken was an Indian called Tomoka John. . . . There were also a number of women and children captured; the former miserable, blackened, haggard, shrivelled (smoke dried and half-clad) devils; the latter ugly little nudities. Although a few guns were fired, this capture was effected without loss or bloodshed on either side.

On questioning the prisoners, we learnt that there was a camp of Uchee Indians among whom was Uchee Billy, their celebrated and formidable chief. . . . Tomoka John offering to guide us to their place of concealment if we would untie him . . . was taken at his word. This Indian led the way in silence for several miles; then gave us to understand that we must perform the rest of the distance on foot, having to pass through a very intricate and extensive cabbage hammock unpassable for horses.

> Taking men with us . . . we started . . . about 4 o'clock in the afternoon. . . . We entered the deep hammock at sunset . . . [and] the darkness of night soon enveloped us. . . . Dividing our force into two columns, . . . we were directed to surround the camp by creeping . . . to the right and left of it; the men in single file and at ten paces apart so as to . . . form a perfect circle around the whole of the enemy. As soon as in position we were to crawl within a hundred yards of the [Indian] fires. . . .

> We succeeded in attaining our assigned positions. . . .

> Twilight with all its shadows and solemn gloom gradually disappeared before the cheerful advent of light, the sky was clear and grayly tinged with the returning light.

> . . . the signal is given; up jump a hundred impatient men . . . and with a shout which "rent heaven's conclave," charged forward at full speed. . . . Instantaneously all the heavens around us were ringing with their horrid war whoop and the clear sharp report of their rifles, blended with the shouts of our men and the louder reports of our carbines. . . . We succeeded in capturing the whole party, which consisted of several warriors with Uchee Billy, and his brother Uchee Jack. . . . One Indian warrior was killed . . . several were wounded . . . Lt. McNeil . . . fell mortally wounded.[8]

At last the troops in Florida, both Regular and volunteer, seemed to be learning the lessons of guerrilla warfare. Philip, Yuchi Billy, and Yuchi Jack were the most important Seminole leaders captured to date.

CHAPTER XIV

Treachery

Duty, Honor, Country

MOTTO OF THE UNITED STATES MILITARY ACADEMY

The failure of General Jesup's peace program continued to rankle. He dispatched letter after bitter letter to Washington, blaming the failure of his plans on everyone but himself. It had been brought about by white traitors, greedy slave-holders, the machinations of Cubans, the treachery of the Creek allies, and the incompetence of Captain William M. Graham, the unfortunate Virginia-born West Pointer, later killed in the Mexican War, who had been in charge of the Indian detention camp at Tampa Bay.

Perhaps more important than placing blame was the impact of the failure on the general himself. Mahon notes that Jesup

. . . with the passage of time became more cynical, more willing to employ treachery to carry out his orders. And since he no longer had confidence in the promises made by Seminoles he

158

felt little compunction about violating his to them. The War now entered a new phase.[1]

General Jesup's feelings went far beyond any mere philosophical distrust of his red and Negro enemies. He coldly concluded that in his future dealings with the Seminole he would disregard all the existing rules of civilized warfare. The depth of Jesup's bitter response to the failure of his peace program and to the criticism that had been heaped upon his head was to lead him into actions he would spend the rest of his life defending. Officers of the American Army had always taken pride in their personal honor. Their word—even to an enemy—had always been their bond. Jesup determined that he would disregard all theoretical questions of gentlemanly conduct. In dealing with savages he would be ruthless—*he* would be savage.

Chief Philip, in captivity, was prevailed upon to send a runner to his son Wildcat, the only one to escape from the Indians' camp near Dunlawton, asking him to come in under a flag of truce. Late in September, in the company of Blue Snake, he came to Fort Payton to see his father. They were bluntly told by the general that, in spite of the white flag, they were under arrest and that if Wildcat were permitted to leave in order to bring in more Indians, his father Philip would be held as a hostage and "would pay" if the son did not return. The young Indian leader was permitted to depart with Tomoka John on October 2 under an agreement to be back in two weeks. He kept his word, returning to St. Augustine on the 17th, bringing with him his uncle and his brother. As a reward, the general clapped him in a dungeon in old Fort Marion. The gloomy old citadel, on which Congress had spent $50,000 for repairs, was considered not only impregnable but escape-proof. It was soon evident that the latter was not true.

Wildcat has been described as "a real Apollo." Although small, he was graceful and agile. When pursued, as at Dunlawton, he not only could outdistance his pursuers, but would often stop to jeer at them before resuming his flight. He is said to have been released under parole for an evening while he was a prisoner at Fort Marion, in order to attend a ball in St. Augustine. Dressed in all his finery, he was lionized at the party. His ideas of gallantry, however, did not meet the standards of the whites. "When introduced to a gentleman and his very pretty new wife he remarked blandly that the young woman was certainly a beauty and that the man no doubt enjoyed her very much, but that after she had a few children she would hardly be worth having."[2]

There are a number of conflicting contemporary accounts of what took place in Fort Marion on the night of November 29, including the highly dramatic story told by Wildcat himself. However, the reconstruction of the events of that evening by the historian Doctor Kenneth W. Porter is probably nearer the truth than are the stories that were told in Florida.

Twenty Indian and Negro Seminole, including two women, were confined in an eighteen-by-thirty-three-foot cell in the southwestern casemate of the fort. The room was lighted by a long, narrow vent about eight inches wide by five feet long. An iron bar ran the length of the window, but it evidently had become eroded and was easily removed. About a foot below the aperture was a ledge that had held ovens when the room had been used as a bakery. With knives they had hidden and kept when captured, the Indians cut up the forage bags given to them for bedding, and made ropes.

The only hitch in the plans of the prisoners occurred when a tipsy guard who visited them wanted to talk and sing. He finally left when they feigned sleep. After he departed, starting with Wildcat, or John Cavallo, an Indian Negro, they squeezed through the window and lowered themselves one by one down the improvised rope to the muddy moat below. They were soon

Co-Ee-Ha-Jo, by George Catlin, 1837

heading south. Moving by night and hiding by day, they eventually made contact with Sam Jones.[3]

The story of the escape soon traveled throughout the Seminole Nation. It served to revive a drooping spirit. As Assistant Surgeon Motte wrote, ". . . the termination of the War we therefore considered as postponed *sine die.*"[4]

While the importance of Wildcat's escape cannot be minimized, it did not have as great an impact on the War as did an incident that occurred a month earlier, near Fort Payton. On October 27, 1837, General Jesup received word that Osceola and Coa Hadjo wanted to meet with the whites in a parley. General Hernandez was directed by Jesup to agree to the council. A spot about a mile south of Fort Payton was agreed upon as the meeting place. Leaving General Jesup at Payton, where he could be handily reached, General Hernandez set out for the talk, with about 250 troops. The escort, commanded by Major James A. Ashby, had previously been instructed to close in and surround the Indians at a given signal.

General Hernandez found Osceola and Coa Hadjo standing under a large white flag so the whites could not misunderstand their peaceful intent. General Jesup had previously given the Indians yards of white cloth so that they could parley with him without fear.[5] Assistant Surgeon Nathan Jarvis, who was present, wrote:

> On our arrival at their camp we discovered at a short distance by a white flag flying the Indians [who] immediately gathered around us shaking hands with all the officers. My attention was of course first directed to discover Os-Cin-Ye-Hola [Osceola]. He was soon pointed out to me but I could have designated him by his looks as the principal man among them. Nothing of savage fierceness or determination marked his countenance, on the contrary his features indicated mildness and benevolence. A continued smile played over his face, particularly when shaking hands with the officers present.[6]

After some talk, General Hernandez, according to Major K. B. Gibbs, the interpreter, asked the Indians, "Have you come to give up to me as your friend?"

Coa Hadjo replied, "No, we did not understand so: word went from here, and we have come; we have done nothing all summer, and we want to make peace." After some additional talk the general gave the signal, and the troops closed in. In addition to Osceola and Coa Hadjo, twelve other Chiefs were taken prisoner, as well as seventy-one warriors, six women, and four Indian Negroes. After the Seminole baggage and forty-seven rifles were collected, horses were provided for Osceola, Coa Hadjo, and the senior of the minor Chiefs. The whole group of prisoners was then marched between a double file of soldiers to St. Augustine and through its streets to Fort Marion.

News of the coup had already reached the city, and most of its citizens were out to catch a glimpse of the famous war chieftain about whom they had heard so much. Assistant Surgeon Jarvis rode beside Osceola the whole distance and reported that while he was obviously unwell, he was in no manner downcast. During the time Osceola was at Fort Marion, he had recurrent fevers, which were probably the result of tertian malaria, which he is said to have contracted at Fort Drane during the summer of 1836. His physician, Doctor Ferry, later said that the Indians, including Osceola, did not seem to regret capture—"their only anxiety was for reunion with their families."

When the story of Osceola's capture and the dishonorable means through which it had been accomplished became known throughout the country, a storm erupted that was almost without parallel. Americans had prided themselves on being the one honest nation in a hostile and corrupt world, and here their representative had committed treachery that even the most perfidious and decadent nations of Europe would have shunned. Jesup's act was denounced by newspapers throughout the country. Meetings condemned this acknowledged act of duplicity. In

Lithograph cartoon I

H. R. Robinson, about 1838-1839

the halls of Congress, the army was damned as having be-
smirched the nation's honor. By a large margin, the House of
Representatives passed a resolution calling on the Secretary of
War to answer ". . . whether any Seminole Indians coming in
under a flag of truce . . . have been made prisoners by General
Jesup."

While Jesup's act unquestionably contributed to the unpopularity of the Van Buren administration and was a factor in the
failure of the Red Fox of Kinderhook's bid for a second term in
1840, its effects were more than just political, for it started one
of the first of the nation's morality sprees. The War in Florida
and the army shared an unpopularity that they had not hitherto
known, and it became fashionable to speak of "the dirty little
war of aggression."

In the process, the uproar was to create a typically American
"Good Guy–Bad Guy" legend. Osceola was the brave and handsome young hero fighting for his homeland against terrific odds,
while Jesup was the old, cowardly villain who would stop at
nothing to accomplish his greedy objective. When it was all
over, three counties, twenty-three towns, two lakes, two moun-
tains, a state park, and a national forest would bear the name of
Osceola.

There were voices raised in behalf of the general. In Congress perhaps as many defended as denounced him. For the
most part, however, their voices were drowned in the clamor.
All kinds of reasons were given for Jesup's actions: Osceola had
broken his word by not taking his people to Tampa the year
before, he had come to Fort Payton to rescue Philip and massacre the whites, he had killed a white messenger under a flag of
truce, and so forth *ad infinitum*. The arguments had little effect.
It is hard to make a convincing argument for immorality—it is
difficult to defend duplicity.

Jesup, of course, spoke out in his own defense and continued to do so for the rest of his life. As late as October 13, 1858, less than two years before his death, he would still be writing to newspapers attempting to justify his perfidy.*

In a long life General Jesup had not learned that honor once besmirched will seldom wash clean or that history never justifies an act of treachery. The best that can charitably be said for Jesup is that he was a humane man who hated the killings in Florida and believed that any action that brought an end to such deaths was justified.

In Florida, however, almost all the settlers praised Jesup as a man of courage who had followed the only course possible. Osceola was a treacherous savage who had been outwitted and skillfully captured. Those in the rest of the country who de-

---

* Under that date in a long letter to the editor of the *Daily Intelligencer* of Washington he said:

> A matter has recently been brought into discussion with which my name was connected some twenty years ago, and though explained at the time, seems not even now to be well understood. It has been published in a neighboring print on the authority of a distinguished professional and public man that the Seminole Indian warrior Osceola who by the murder of General Thompson and other atrocities started the Seminole War, "was captured by treachery and fraud."
>
> In a conference which I held with the Seminole Chiefs . . . but a few weeks before, I had assured them that I would hold no further conferences with them except to receive from them the notice of their readiness to fulfill their obligations under the treaty of Paynes' Landing. . . .
>
> The chiefs expressed some apprehension that in coming to me they might be attacked by my scouting parties, and their people be scattered. To enable them to join me without danger of attack from these parties, I provided them with a quantity of white cotton cloth, to be used as flags in communicating with any of those parties they might fall in with, and with my outposts; but the flags were to be used for no other purpose. And the chiefs were distinctly and positively told that none of them nor their people must attempt to come in again but to remain.

nounced the general were bleeding hearts, do-gooders, or Indian-
and Negro-lovers. Only among army officers was there any
considerable group on the peninsula who outspokenly criticized
the general's actions.

In St. Augustine there was concern as to the wisdom of
bringing the Chiefs to the city for imprisonment. Might not the
Seminole attempt to free Osceola and in the process kill the
town's inhabitants? The War Department evidently agreed, for
it shipped the prisoners, under heavy guard, to Charleston,
on January 1, 1838.

In Charleston the Indian prisoners were treated almost as
visiting royalty. In prison they were allowed to receive visitors,
and it became fashionable to take the trip to Fort Moultrie and
call on Osceola.

On invitation of the War Department, George Catlin arrived in Charleston on January 17, and the Chief sat for his
portrait. The former Philadelphia lawyer and self-taught
painter* was impressed by the warrior, and his later glowing
descriptions contributed to the growing Osceola legend.

On January 6, 1838, the New Theatre proudly advertised in
the *Courier:* "This evening . . . OSCEOLA and the other
INDIAN CHIEFS will be in attendance." The Chiefs were
present and witnessed the performance of a play called "Honey-
Moon." In the same issue an editorial admonished:

. . . We have heard within a day or two, very bitter things
said of OSCEOLA by a few persons. In our humble opinion, he
has been to the full, as much sinned against as sinning. Treacherous he may have been, but we cannot forget that he was provoked
by treachery, and captured by treachery. We are fairly even with
him. We now owe him the respect which the brave ever feel
toward the brave; which the victorious cannot violate without

---

* Catlin's 479 portraits of Indians, including a number of the Seminole,
many of which are now in the collection of the Smithsonian Institution, have placed him among the foremost of American artists.

brutality towards the vanquished, which the commonest laws of humanity and civilization enforce towards prisoners of war. We sincerely trust that no citizen of Charleston will so far forget the character of a Carolinian, as to offer indignity to a fallen man. A tear of forgiveness and generous sympathy is much better due to the once terrible, now stricken warriors of the Seminoles.

It was a far cry from those days in 1836 when the Charleston Militia, in their resplendent uniforms and carrying lovingly hand-stitched flags, proudly marched off to avenge the victims of Dade's Massacre and the murder of General Wiley Thompson.

Osceola had been joined at Fort Marion by his two wives, two of their children, a sister, three warriors, and about forty Negro retainers. They went with him to Moultrie and did their best to make him as comfortable as possible.

In spite of the care he was given, Osceola's health grew worse at Fort Moultrie. It did not help when he refused the services of Doctor Frederick Weedon, the post surgeon, and insisted rather on the ministrations of a medicine man. On January 27, it appeared that he was dying, and George Catlin and a group of officers sat up with him. He rallied, and on the 29th, when Catlin left for Philadelphia, he appeared on the way to recovery. The next day, however, he began to sink rapidly. Realizing that the end was near, he insisted that he be dressed in his finest array. That evening in the presence of his wives, two of his children, and several of the officers, he died. His death was attributed to malaria and acute quinsy.

Osceola was buried the next day near the main entrance of the fort, with full military honors. The funeral was attended by all the Indian prisoners, a number of officers of the post, and a large delegation of Charleston residents. His grave was enclosed by a plain fence, and, some time later, a Mr. Patton, a Charlestonian, erected a marble headstone:

OSCEOLA

Patriot and Warrior
Died at Fort Moultrie
January 30th, 1838.[7]

Osceola was to do as much in death for the Seminole Nation
as he had during his life. He had died at the right time for the
perpetuation of a legend. That he had fought cleanly, had not
killed women and children, had not mutilated the dead or tor-
tured prisoners was remembered; that he had killed unmerci-
fully and without compunction was forgotten. After his death he
became the embodiment of the noble red man who had fought
and died for his people, for his homeland: a symbol of the best
in man. Thereafter, the opposition to the War throughout the
country solidified. The conflict became known for what it was, a
war of aggression.

In death Osceola was treated by the press as a national hero.
There were glowing elegies and flowery tributes to the young
chieftain. Perhaps the best of these appeared in *Niles National
Register* on February 2, 1838:

> We shall not write his epitaph or his funeral orations, yet
> there is something in his character not unworthy of the respect
> of the world. From a vagabond child he became the master spirit
> of a long and desperate war. He made himself—no man owed
> less to accident. Bold and decisive in action, deadly but consistent
> in hatred, dark in revenge, cool, subtle and sagacious in council,
> he established gradually and surely a resistless ascendancy over
> his adoptive tribe, by the daring of his deeds, and the consistency
> of his hostility to the whites, and the profound craft of his policy.
> In council he spoke little—he made the other chiefs his instru-
> ments, and what they delivered in public was the secret suggestion
> of the invisible master. Such was Osceola who will be long re-
> membered as the man that with the feeblest means produced the
> most terrible effects.*

---

* Mark F. Boyd, a leading authority on Osceola, has called this "The
best contemporary appraisal of Osceola we have encountered."

The high regard for the dead Indian leader was of course not unanimous, and the degradation of Osceola was to continue after death. The body buried at Fort Moultrie was not intact: it had been decapitated. Doctor Frederick Weedon, who had attended Osceola at forts Marion and Moultrie, had originally come to Florida as a colonel in Jackson's Army. Practicing medicine in St. Augustine, he became the civilian physician for Fort Marion. Subsequently he married Mary Thompson, the sister of Indian agent Wiley Thompson, whom Osceola later murdered.

Following the Indian's death, Doctor Weedon was alone with the corpse, and he seized the opportunity to sever the head from the body, which he concealed by the Indian's scarf. Then when he performed his assigned task of closing Osceola's coffin, he first removed the head, later taking it with him to his home on Bridge Street in St. Augustine.* Although he justified his actions on scientific grounds, the decapitation must also be viewed as an act of vengeance.

In October 1837, there emerged from the War Department a plan that was hoped would win the War. The Cherokee settled in the West had long been friends of the Seminole. Why not send a delegation of their Chiefs to Florida to tell the Seminole of the abundant life beyond the Mississippi? Perhaps In-

---

* He was said to have used the head to frighten his sons when they were disobedient.

After his daughter married a physician, Doctor Daniel Whitehurst of New York, Weedon gave the head to his new son-in-law. Perhaps it was a wedding gift. Whitehurst in turn gave the head to Doctor Valentine Mott, one of the foremost surgeons of his day and one of the founders of the New York University School of Medicine. Doctor Mott in turn placed the head in his Surgical and Pathological Museum, with a card identifying it as the head of Osceola and a gift of Doctor Whitehurst. In 1866 the museum caught fire, and part of the collection, including the head, was destroyed.[8]

dians could succeed with their fellow red men where white men had failed.

The Cherokee arrived at St. Augustine in November and first asked for permission to talk with the Indian prisoners in Fort Marion. Jesup gave his grudging consent, but specified that on such a visit there should be white officers present at all times.

Word had come from Micanopy that he would meet with the delegation at Fort Mellon. Jesup was reluctant to have the Cherokee go, insisting that any negotiations would delay his fall campaign for weeks, but he finally gave in, insisting, however, that the Chiefs travel the fifty miles to Mellon, confer with Micanopy, and return within six days.

Like so many plans put into operation during the Seminole War, the program met with initial success. The delegation was back on the sixth day, and with it came Micanopy, Yaholoochee and eleven sub-Chiefs. Unfortunately the Indians thought they had come to negotiate under a flag of truce and a guarantee of safe conduct, as they had been promised by the Cherokee. They were soon to learn that this was not General Jesup's understanding.

The delegation of western Indians again left St. Augustine for Fort Mellon in early December, but this time the Cherokee were unable to convince either Sam Jones or Wildcat to return with them. The two Seminole just laughed at them, and the former charged them with being traitors. General Jesup's reaction when the Cherokee reported their failure was characteristic. He clapped Micanopy and those with him into Fort Marion as prisoners of war. The Cherokee delegation's insistence that their good word was at stake did not impress the general. The Cherokee Chiefs were wiser men when they left Florida for their home beyond the Mississippi.

General Jesup now had in his hands most of the leaders of the Seminole Nation: he felt that the tribe should now be easy prey for his troops in the campaign he was about to launch.

CHAPTER XV

The Winter Campaign of 1837-1838

[We are] almost eaten up by fleas, ants, cockroaches, and almost all manner of vermin.

CAPTAIN JOSEPH SMITH, 1838

I n spite of his distaste for citizen-soldiers, General Jesup spent the summer months of 1837 calling on the states for volunteers. He did not expect that half the troops he asked for would arrive, but by mid-fall he found himself with an embarrassment of riches.

To begin with, he had more Regulars than any of his predecessors. The army at that time numbered 7,130 men, and of these 4,636 (including the detachment of 170 marines) were serving in Florida.

In September volunteer and militia troops began to flood the Territory. Besides the Florida Volunteers, there were large bodies of men from Georgia, Alabama, Louisiana, and Tennessee. Two companies came from Pennsylvania, and one each from New York and the District of Columbia. Altogether Jesup had a total of a little over 4,000 citizen-soldiers. Including the

Regulars, his army thus totaled almost 9,000 men, many times more than he could support in the field. In addition, in the late fall a regiment arrived from Missouri. Through illness and desertion, however, the First Missouri Volunteers, originally 600 strong, were reduced to 180 troops before they saw combat.

General Jesup's plans for the winter campaign were entirely different from those that had previously been used in Florida. Gone was the classical synchronized pincer movement of two or three large armies. Instead there would be seven separate and relatively small forces which acting on their own would have the mission of seeking and destroying the enemy in a specified area. As far as possible, each would be self-sufficient and establish its own supply points.

Colonel Zachary Taylor, commander of the army formed at Fort Brooke, commanded a brigade composed of his own First [Regular] Infantry Regiment, the depleted Missouri Regiment, elements of the Fourth and Sixth Infantries, and a newly formed outfit called "Morgan's Spies," composed of Delaware and Shawnee Indians. Altogether Taylor had about 1,000 men to cover a zone between the Kissimmee River and Pease Creek. Lieutenant Levy N. Powell, USN, with eighty-five sailors, two companies of artillery and a company of militia, would penetrate the Everglades. Colonel Persifor F. Smith, marching inland from the mouth of the Coloosahatchee River with 600 Louisiana Volunteers, would seek out the Indians in an area south of that covered by Colonel Taylor. The rest of the 400 troops in the field would be divided into four columns, all advancing toward the headwaters of the St. Johns River. General Hernandez would start out from Mosquito Lagoon with his Florida Militia; Colonel John Warren would go southward between the Atlantic Ocean and the St. Johns River with two companies of dragoons and Florida Militia; General Eustis, leading a mixed force of volunteers and miscellaneous other troops, would cover the area between Fort King and the Oklawaha River. The bal-

ance of General Jesup's excess of troops would be used in garrison duty and in the northern zone of the interior. General Armistead, who had been ill but had returned to duty, was named
Deputy Theatre Commander.

Taylor's force left Fort Brooke on December 2. About forty
miles due east of Tampa they built a small stockade, which was
called Fort Frazer. Another post, Fort Gardner, was established
south of Cypress Swamp on the Kissimmee River. Taylor hoped
to protect his lines of communication by leaving small garrisons
and supplies at each of the new forts.

As the troops traveled south, the going became rough, and
on December 21 Taylor established Fort Bessinger on the Kissimmee River, about forty-five miles south of Fort Gardner.
There he left a detachment of a company, eighty-five men who
were on the sick list, some friendly Indians, and all his heavy
baggage and artillery.

Almost from the start of Taylor's campaign small parties of
Seminole came in to surrender. The largest of these groups
included Jumper and sixty-three of his followers. On the 22nd,
when their camp was discovered by soldiers, another twenty-
three gave up. On the 24th Taylor's troops found a large deserted Seminole camp in which the fires were still burning. It
was destroyed.

About mid-morning on Christmas Day, the troops captured a
single warrior, a brother-in-law of Negro leader John Cavallo,
who, it appears, was a decoy. He told them that the enemy were
in a hammock running approximately north and south along
Lake Okeechobee. It was one of the strongest positions the
Seminole had ever taken. With Lake Okeechobee to their rear,
and a half-mile sawgrass swamp, in which the mud and water
were three feet deep, on their front, some 450 warriors awaited
the attack of the whites. More than half of the red men, under
old Sam Jones, were concentrated on the right of the hammock;
Alligator and 120 braves held the center; Wildcat and 80 of

his followers were on the left. Unfortunately for the Indians, there was no concentration of Negroes with them—just a small group lead by John Cavallo.

After a conference with his officers, Taylor proposed a frontal attack on the Seminole center. Gentry, according to the Missourians, suggested an encirclement, whereupon Taylor rather briskly asked if he were afraid, and stuck to his original plan. The First Missouri Regiment and Morgan's Spies were to be in the first line of attack, followed by the Fourth and Sixth Infantries, with the First in reserve.

The first line started the advance through the swamp at twelve-thirty P.M. Almost immediately it took on heavy fire, and Colonel Gentry was mortally wounded. It was too much for the Missouri Volunteers, and, according to Taylor and Lieutenant Robert C. Buchanan, they broke in disorder, went to the rear, and thereafter were out of the battle.[1] The Fourth and Sixth Infantries, however, continued the advance. Colonel Ramsey Thompson, commander of the five companies of the Sixth Regiment, received a fatal wound. Propped up against a tree, he called out to his men, "Remember the regiment to which you belong," and died. When all but one officer and most of the noncoms had become casualties, the Sixth withdrew to the rear and re-formed.

Taylor next ordered his reserve to the Indians' right and hit them in the flank. As the fresh troops advanced, the Indians fired a final volley and began to withdraw to the east. There were so many casualties to be evacuated that the Indians were not pursued. By three P.M. the battle was over.

The Seminole had been driven from their prepared position, but at a terrific price. Taylor had suffered twenty-six killed and 112 wounded. The red men had had eleven warriors killed and suffered fourteen wounded.

To move the wounded and dead from the swamp, it was necessary to build a footway, and it was not until the afternoon of the 26th that all of the injured had received care and the dead had been buried. The next day, with his wounded carried on rude stretchers made of poles and steer hides, Taylor moved out, arriving at Fort Gardner on the last day of the year. From there the wounded, under escort of the Fourth and Sixth Infantries, were taken by wagon to Fort Brooke.

Colonel Taylor's troops were not the only ones to breathe the acrid smell of gunpowder during the holiday season. On the day after Christmas, far to the north, along the Wacasassa River, Major General Charles H. Nelson and 600 of his Georgia Volunteers ran into a wandering band of Indians. A brisk engagement ensued. Several soldiers and an undetermined number of warriors were killed, but the bulk of the braves were again able to escape.

Naval Lieutenant Powell and his hodge-podge collection of 200 sailors and soldiers also took part in several small skirmishes with the enemy. Assistant Surgeon Motte, while camped between the Indian River and Mosquito Lagoon, saw Powell's unit. He described it as presenting

> . . . a curious blending of black and white, like the keys of a piano forte; many of the sailors being colored men. There was also an odd alternation of tarpaulin hats and pea jackets, with forage caps and soldiers' trim roundabouts; soldiers and sailors, white men and black, being all thrown into the ranks indiscriminately, a beautiful specimen of mosaic; thus modifying sailor's ardor with soldier's discipline.[2]

The most serious of Powell's engagements with the Indians occurred on January 15. Near the head of the Jupiter River they found a fresh trail and, following it, came on a large herd of cattle and horses tended by a squaw. Forcing her to guide them to the nearby Seminole encampment, they discovered the Indians at the head of a cypress swamp. With no knowledge of the terrain or the strength of the hostiles, the troops charged the enemy. They were met by devastating fire, and a number of the sailors who were greenhorns broke and ran. The remaining sailors and soldiers stood firm and covered the panic-stricken. It was four o'clock in the afternoon when the action started, and it was not until seven-thirty that the force regained its boats. All of the officers except a Mr. Johnson, acting adjutant of the detachment, were wounded.

Meanwhile, General Jesup himself had not been inactive. Joining the St. Johns Brigade, he ordered a fort constructed at a point about eighty miles north of the Lake Okeechobee battleground. It was intended as a supply depot and was named Fort Christmas, because of the date on which the work was started. It was finished in five days, and on January 3 Jesup moved south, with the temperature at 103 degrees in the sun. Both men and horses wilted in the unseasonable heat, and the going was correspondingly slow.

Jesup was not the only one to construct forts. Taylor's men established Fort Floyd, about twelve miles above the Okeechobee battleground; the Tennessee Volunteers built Fort Lauderdale at the source of the New River; and on the Atlantic, almost a hundred miles to the north of Fort Lauderdale, Fort Pierce was constructed on Indian River Inlet, directly across the peninsula from Tampa Bay.

On January 18 the St. Johns force, led by Jesup, made contact with Taylor's troops some twenty miles west of Fort Floyd. Continuing south, the general's men passed the site of Lieutenant Powell's battle, where they searched without success for the body of Naval Surgeon Doctor Leitner.

The St. Johns River Brigade continued through wild, trackless, unmapped country. In his *Journal*, Doctor Motte described the march:

> The next day we crossed the headwater of the St. Lucie River; floundering through mud and water for a mile and a half

up to our saddle flaps in depth. On emerging from this swamp on the south side, we came upon the site of an extensive Indian camp, which presented signs of having been recently abandoned. . . . Our route all this day lay through submerged scrub flats, and saw palmetto swells, interspersed with cypress and bay ponds. These ponds generally exhibited in their centre picturesque clumps of cypress trees and willows, ornamentally clothed with long hanging moss, gracefully and fantastically disposed in festoons, forming fairy looking islets reposing in verdant loveliness on the bosom of the water, and so nearly level with it, as to appear floating upon its shining surface; fit abodes for the genii of these unearthly regions, which come nearest the description of that fabulous place, that we read of, which was neither land, water, or air. Indeed, the whole country, since leaving Fort Pierce, had been one unbroken extent of water and morass; a very little land; much saw-palmetto; and more snakes, mosquitoes, and other venomous critters than one can shake a stick at.

On January 24 the march was renewed, with the water ". . . nearly up to the men's waists; many of whom were barefooted, their clothes torn off, and flesh badly lacerated by the saw-palmetto."[3] At twelve noon, Captain William M. Fulton, whose company of dragoons was serving as the advance guard, reported that the hostiles, who were strongly positioned in a dense hammock ahead, had fired on his men. Jesup ordered the dragoons to attack, with the support of the artillerymen. To reach the hammock it was necessary to cross a deep cypress slough. In waist-deep water the dragoons dismounted and moved forward to the accompaniment of the sharp blasts of the six-pounders and the whiz of the Congreve rockets. General Jesup, leading a second wave of the Tennessee Volunteers, was hit in the cheek by a bullet and his glasses were smashed. After carefully picking up his shattered spectacles, he waved the men forward and moved to the aid station at the rear.

Having gained the hammock, the troops found that the enemy had withdrawn across a deep, thirty-foot-wide stream.

Not knowing of the ford the Indians had used, many of the men floundered into water, got beyond their depth, and were forced to swim, their ammunition becoming wet. Fortunately, however, after the soldiers had gained the far shore, the Seminole withdrew and the Battle of Locksahatchee came to an end. Seven whites had died and thirty-one, including Jesup, were wounded. A number of the wounded later died. It was noted by Motte that the hostile force had been composed of from 200 to 300 braves, about equally divided between Indians and Negroes.

Motte's description of the field after the battle is vivid:

> We recrossed the Locha-Hatchee to the north side; and encamped upon the battle field. Many of the soldiers were employed in collecting the killed and wounded; and bringing them to the foot of a spreading oak, beneath whose wildly flung branches were strewn a score of dead and dying. There before us lay death in his most horrible forms; bodies pierced with ghastly wounds, and locks begrimed with gore. In one direction, leaning against a tree, there reclined a soldier of the Artillery; his face pale, and o'spread with an expression of anguish; one hand pressed to his side, from which blood slowly oozed. In another direction lay stretched upon the ground, with face turned upward, and glazed eyes wide open, one whose marble cheek too plainly told that the rifle ball which had entered his temple had truly done its mission; —that he "slept a sleep that knows no waking."[4]

The men of the St. Johns Brigade were now in ragged condition. Jesup, even as a quartermaster, had had his comeuppance. Over 400 of his men were actually barefooted. There was obviously no other alternative than to bivouac his troops at a spot he called Fort Jupiter, on Jupiter Inlet, and wait for a shipment of shoes. They were also out of forage and had but two days' rations left. Fortunately Major Edmund Kirby and the First Artillery arrived by barges on the 27th, bringing needed supplies, but no shoes.

On the 5th, foot gear and other supplies having arrived, Jesup and his command set out again. On the 7th they came to a cypress swamp where scouts reported the presence of the Seminole. This time, however, before attacking, the general sent a message by an Indian Negro, Sandy, offering the hostiles peace and inviting the Chiefs to a conference. At about midday a delegation of Indians under a white flag was seen advancing from the swamp. A young Chief, Halleck Hadjo, told the general that the tribes were in wretched condition, their cattle and ponies gone and the women and children dying, from the hardships of "being chased about so much," and that above all they wanted peace but earnestly prayed that they might remain in Florida. They would "thankfully receive the smallest piece of ground that might be given to them, no matter how bad, if it only was in Florida, and big enough for them to spread their blankets upon." General Jesup for once seemed moved, but he requested that they return the next day with Tuskegee, their principal Chief, and they agreed to do so.

In mid-morning of the following day, Tuskegee and a large suite arrived at Jesup's encampment. After again listening to the Indians, the general agreed to recommend to Washington that they be permitted to remain in Florida. Jesup told Tuskegee that his troops would return to Fort Jupiter, and the Chief agreed that he would bring his people there within ten days, to wait for the President's decision.

The troops started back to Jupiter on the 10th, and they arrived there the next day. True to his promise, General Jesup immediately set to work on a letter to Poinsett. There had never been an instance, he wrote the Secretary, in which the Indians had been pushed out before the land they held was needed by white men. The Seminole, he noted, were not now in the way of the white settlers' advance in Florida. If immediate immigration west were insisted upon, the War in Florida could drag on for years. The message was dispatched by hand to Washington, carried by Jesup's aide, Lieutenant Thomas B. Linnard.

The Indians kept their promise and within a few days were encamped within a mile of Fort Jupiter. Altogether, there were about 400 warriors, including many Negroes.

On February 24, the red men, "cutting the most fantastic capers," put on a ceremony in which Tuskegee, Halleck, and Halleck Hadjo, dressed in their best finery, led the braves into the soldiers' camp. Reaching the general's tent, they smoked a calumet. Thereafter, the red men shook elbows with each of the white officers, touching them with a white feather on a stick. Motte was impressed by the Indians, but noted that the Negroes "were the most diabolical-looking wretches I ever saw; their style of dress contributing much to render them voracious and Oriental in aspect. They had none of the servility of our northern blacks, but were constantly offering their dirty paws with as much hauteur, and nonchalance, as if they were conferring a vast deal of honour, of which we should have been proud."[5]

Word did not come from Washington until St. Patrick's Day. In no uncertain words Jesup was told that the Indians could not remain in Florida. The general did not hesitate. In total disregard for the flag of truce, the Seminole camp was surrounded by the Second Dragoons, and over 500 Indians and Negroes, including 150 warriors, were disarmed and made prisoners. What General Jesup could not achieve on the battlefield, he could at least accomplish by treachery.

Meanwhile, Colonel, now Brevet Brigadier General, Taylor had not been inactive, having bagged Holatoochee and forty warriors. Jesup was delighted.

Ever since the abortive truce of March 1837, Abraham had been the general's prisoner, and on April 3, holding their families as hostages for their return, Jesup sent the Negro leader and Holatoochee to Alligator to induce him to give up the fight. They were able to convince the formidable chieftain of the futility of continuing the conflict, and he surrendered four days later. Alligator brought with him to captivity eighty-eight others, including John Cavallo and twenty-seven of his Negro followers.

Not all of the Seminole, however, were so acquiescent. In late March, leading a detachment of Taylor's force, Lieutenant Colonel James Bankhead of the Fourth Artillery stumbled on a group of hostiles in the usual defensive position, on the edge of a hammock. Bankhead tried for a three-way envelopment. With two companies in position in the center facing the Indians, he sent a detachment through waist-high water to the left, while a mixed detail of sailors and soldiers in rowboats was dispatched to the right. The latter force had a four-pounder which could be fired from its barge. It seemed a good plan, but the Indians, when they saw what was happening, simply withdrew to the rear and melted away.

Despite the lack of success of his troops in combat, General Jesup, who by nature was an optimist, next determined to take Sam Jones. Lieutenant Colonel William Selby Harney of the Second Dragoons was assigned the task. Harney, a native of Louisiana who would retire as a brigadier general, was six feet, three inches tall and wore a cavalryman's mustache and a full beard. The Colonel was one of those men who could command by his mere presence. Though he had been in Florida since 1836, he still, like many of his southern contemporaries, viewed all but whites as inferior beings.

In his new assignment, Harney set to work with gusto. After picking out fifty of his dragoons, who were armed with the new Colt rifles, and fifty men from the Third Artillery with muskets, he set out from Fort Lauderdale on April 15. Doctor Motte was the detachment's surgeon. From a point Harney called Camp Center, which had been established at the mouth of the Miami River, a few miles south of Fort Dallas, the troops embarked in fifteen log canoes and proceeded south.

On April 24, not far south of Cape Florida, but on the

mainland, they left the boats. Passing through a sawgrass prairie, they struck a trail that led to a recently deserted Indian camp. Continuing, the detachment reached a pine barren where jutting coral tore through the men's shoes, lacerating their feet. Motte could not understand how the Indians in their moccasins could travel over such ground, until he learned that they made their footgear of alligator hide.

At about one o'clock in the afternoon, Harney's detail heard distant shouting. Going on, they came in sight of the smoke from Indian campfires. The troops had found the camp of old Sam Jones.

Harney divided his force into three detachments and ordered a charge on the village. The warriors, taken completely by surprise, grabbed their arms and took positions behind trees to protect the withdrawal of the women and children. They were soon able to stop the oncoming whites and force them also to seek protection. Gradually, after their noncombatants had been able to get away, the braves began a slow withdrawal. After two and a half hours they broke off action and took off through the woods. The troopers pursued, but became so divided in small groups of two or three men that Colonel Harney, fearful of their being attacked in fragments, had recall sounded. The engagement had been a disappointment. Only one warrior had been killed and only one woman captured.

That evening Harney and his men, after eating coontie and venison left by the Indians, made camp for the night. The next day the weary men returned to their boats. On the morning of the 29th, they returned to Camp Center.

Somehow a number of small bands of Indians had avoided Jesup's troops and made their way back north. In late March and during April they murdered a number of civilians in the St. Johns River sugar area. General Jesup immediately dispatched General Armistead to take command there. General Eustis was sent to take over the Suwannee region.

In Washington, Congress had become restless over the conduct of the War. Altogether, the conflict was costing over $450,000 a month, for a grand total of $9,400,000 to date. The debate in Congress was almost entirely along sectional lines. In the House, Caleb Cushing thundered that Andy Jackson's War had cost the nation this colossal sum; William K. Bond charged that the War, in preventing the payment of installments of the Federal surplus, was holding up domestic improvements; John Quincy Adams of Massachusetts asserted that his state received no benefit from these military expenditures; Henry A. Wise of Virginia called the War a disgrace, condemning General Jesup's treacherous seizure of Osceola; and Richard Biddle of Pennsylvania said he would vote for no more military expenditures until he learned how the money was being spent. In both houses there were calls for an investigation of the conduct of the War.

In Florida, General Jesup longed for the peace and quiet of his quartermaster office back in Washington. He asked to be relieved. On April 29, the answer arrived. As soon as matters in Florida could be arranged, he was free to return and resume his Washington duties as Quartermaster General. He set to work with a will, and on May 15 he turned over the command to General Zachary Taylor and left for the North. General Jesup had had enough.

CHAPTER XVI

"Old Rough and Ready"

> The Government is in the wrong, and this
> is the chief cause of the persevering opposition
> of the Indians, who have nobly defended their
> country against our attempt to enforce a fraud-
> ulent treaty.
>
> MAJOR ETHAN ALLEN HITCHCOCK, 1839

None of the commanders in Florida, with the possible exception of Zachary Taylor, came out of the War with an
enhanced reputation. Taylor's reputation stemmed more from
the Battle of Okeechobee than from his conduct of the army. A
Virginian whose family moved to Kentucky while he was yet a
boy, he was almost without formal schooling. Fifty-four years
old at the time he assumed command, he nevertheless had the
vigor of youth. Although he had entered the army as a lieutenant in 1808, the same year as Clinch, Scott, and Jesup,[1] most
of his service had been on the western frontiers, where promotion had been hard to come by, and he did not become a colonel
until April 4, 1832. He became a brigadier by brevet following
Okeechobee. He had served in the Black Hawk War, but before
Florida had never commanded more than a regiment.

Profane, brusque to the point of being discourteous, but ac-

General Zachary Taylor

cessible, Taylor was much admired by the enlisted men, who called him "Old Rough and Ready." Seldom in uniform, he disliked the formalities of the military. He was a strict disciplinarian, but fair and certainly not a martinet. He was, of course, eventually to become President of the United States.

When he took command in Florida, the Army of the South, as it was now called, was at its lowest strength level since the start of the War. It comprised only 2,300 men, all but 467 being Regulars. The term of the other volunteers had expired, and they had gone home.

Lack of manpower, however, did not seem to deter Taylor, for he also had no high opinion of citizen-soldiers. He considered one Regular worth a dozen militiamen. Only a few days after relieving Jesup, he wrote Governor Call that he intended to discontinue the use of volunteers during the summer months—"the sickly season," as it was then called in Florida. He would rely, he said, on his thirty companies of Regulars. Militia Brigadier General Call was not pleased.

The governor also took a dim view of the rest of Taylor's letter. With his Regulars, Taylor wrote, he would drive the hostiles south of a line running roughly from St. Augustine to Garey's Ferry and thence down the old military road from Fort King to south of Tampa. This, "Old Rough and Ready" added, would push the Seminole away from "every portion of Florida worth protecting." Call exploded. In his opinion much more of Florida was worth protecting than the portion Taylor had suggested.

General Taylor's determination to use only Regulars did, however, elicit a favorable response in Washington. It was right along the lines of Secretary of War Poinsett's thinking, for it would cut down Federal expenditures, and Congress was becoming restless over the cost of the War. On June 1, the War Department set a limit of 1,000 on the number of militia that could be called to Federal service.

Meanwhile, engagements with the Seminole continued. On May 28, 1838, a party of about twenty warriors penetrated north and attacked an element of forty Florida Militia on the Georgia border, about a mile from the Okefenokee Swamp. The militiamen suffered two casualties. On June 4 a sharp but inconclusive skirmish was fought in heavy rain between a detachment of dragoons and a mixed band of Indians and Negroes on the Withlacoochee River, near Clinch's former battleground. The Regulars had to abandon pursuit after suffering heavy casualties. Somewhat later, hostiles burned Fort Dade and again tried to destroy the log bridge across the Withlacoochee. Captain Walker, a Newnansville Militia officer, was killed and six dragoons were wounded during a skirmish on the Kanapaha prairie.

In mid-July hostiles operating out of the Okefenokee Swamp murdered several Georgia families. Later in the month, a family named Gwinns, living on the Santa Fe River, were killed. The Gwinns baby, after its brains were bashed out, was put in its dead mother's arms. On July 28 another family, the Lesleys, were murdered near Tallahassee.

Governor Call now concluded that his opposition to the reduction in the number of volunteer troops had been justified. The Regulars could not do the job alone. With the expectation that Secretary Poinsett would be forced to induct them into Federal service, he ordered to duty three companies of mounted Florida Militia. He was correct, for the Secretary began to soften his volunteer policy. On August 20 he directed Taylor to issue a call for 500 mounted Floridians for the defense of Middle Florida. The general's opinion of citizen-soldiers had not improved, and he practically ignored Poinsett's instructions. He did authorize subordinate commanders to enroll militia, if necessary.

Action to end the depredations had to be taken, and Taylor proposed to the War Department that the area from the Withlacoochee River north through North Florida be laid off in twenty-mile squares. A small blockhouse garrisoning about twenty men would be located in the center of each square. The commanding officer was to build roads and trails around and throughout the square over which there would be daily patrols thereafter. While Taylor's square plan was not favorably received by the press in the Territory, on September 15 he received approval for it from the War Department. He immediately set to work putting the program into operation.

Meanwhile, Taylor continued Jesup's policy of negotiating with any Indians who were willing to parley. The remaining Apalachicola agreed to turn themselves in for western migration by October 1, and did so. Taylor was not so successful with the Tallahassee, who agreed to go west, but failed to keep their bargain.

The general also set into operation a program to more rapidly send to the West those Seminole who came into his hands. Marine Lieutenant John G. Reynolds was put in charge of the operation. Reynolds' principal worry was not, however, the Indians, but rather the knotty Negro problem.

General Taylor, though a Southerner and a slaveholder, was nevertheless much more compassionate on the subject of the Indian Negroes than any of his predecessors had been. While he promised to return any slave to his or her rightful legal owner, he insisted he would not "aid in depriving the Seminoles of their Negroes nor would he do anything that would reduce the latter from comparative freedom to slavery." Lieutenant Reynolds found his path strewn with obstacles when he tried to carry out the policy of his commanding general.

The Creek had a claim on some seventy Negroes who were being shipped west along with a contingent of over 1,000 Seminole Indians and Negroes. They sold the claim for $15,000 to a James C. Watson of Georgia. Watson sent his brother-in-law, Nathaniel F. Collins, to New Orleans, where the group was awaiting shipment to Arkansas, to take possession of his purchase. Backed by General Gaines, again in command at New Orleans, Lieutenant Reynolds refused to release the Negroes. When hailed into court by Collins, the general testified that all Negroes in his possession were prisoners of war and could not be released to anyone. With Collins threatening everyone within sight and damning the military, the entire consignment of both Indians and Negroes was loaded on a steamboat and dispatched to distant Fort Gibson. Collins followed, catching up with the shipment at Vicksburg.

Meanwhile, both Indian Commissioner C. A. Harris and Secretary of War Joel Poinsett intervened on behalf of Collins. Reynolds was directed to turn over possession of the seventy Negroes. But by now Collins' actions had put the Indians aboard the ship in a near-mutinous state. Reynolds and the other officers just ignored the Secretary's order, and the expedition continued westward.

Reynolds' career was in a precarious position. At Little Rock he had no other alternative but to call on the governor of the Territory for sufficient militia to seize the seventy Negroes by force. The governor, however, wanted no part of the proceedings. Denouncing the actions taken, he announced that had the government

> . . . intended to dispose of these Negroes to the Creek Indians, it should have been done in Florida, and not bring [Seminole] and Negroes into Arkansas . . . then irritate the Indians to madness; and turn them loose on our frontier, where we have no adequate protection—the massacre of our citizens would be the inevitable consequence.

While Lieutenant Reynolds was delighted by the governor's action, he felt called upon to make the same request to Fort Gibson's commander, General Matthew Arbuckle, but the latter also declined to move. Reynolds was thus able to deliver to their destination over 1,200 Indian and Negro Seminole.[2] Collins, a frustrated but wiser man, returned to Georgia.

Meanwhile, General Jesup had arrived in Washington and resumed his duties as Quartermaster General. Almost his first action after his return was to send Major Truman Cross, who had been Acting QG in the general's absence, south to become quartermaster in Florida. Cross was directed to put an austerity program into effect in the Army of the South. Civilian agents, clerks, and laborers were to be discharged from their posts, with their places assumed by the military. The number of mounts was to be reduced, and ambulances were to be used only for carrying the sick and wounded. The resulting clamor, raised principally by the discharged civilians, was to make Jesup even more disliked in Florida.

In November, with the arrival of cool weather, Taylor arranged the disposition of his command for the winter months. He hoped to drive the Seminole below a line stretching from New Smyrna to Fort Brooke. He planned a new road from one end of the line to the other. There was to be a strong post every twenty miles. Lieutenant Colonel David E. Twiggs, a Georgian, was directed to erect a new post and cover the area between the St. Johns River and the Atlantic Ocean as far south as New Smyrna with a detachment of the Second Dragoons. Lieutenant Colonel William Davenport, a Pennsylvanian, with elements of the First Infantry, was to reactivate Fort Clinch and police the country between there and the mouth of the Withlacoochee River. Lieutenant Colonel John Greene, a native of Ireland who had entered the army in 1812, leading a detail of the Sixth Infantry, was responsible for the area between the St. Johns and the Suwannee Rivers. Major Gustavus Loomis, a Vermonter and a West Point graduate in the class of 1811, with a mixed force of Regulars and militiamen, was assigned the Okefenokee sector. Finally, Lieutenant Colonel Fanning was directed to re-establish Fort Mellon on Lake George.

In spite of all Taylor's efforts, Indians continued to murder settlers. In one week alone, twelve white men were killed. It was impossible to cover the entire Territory with the limited number of troops the general had at his command. When his soldiers, after receiving word of Indian activity, arrived at a burned and devastated farm, the Indians had long since gone.

Taylor, because of his refusal to use militia, was blamed by the Floridians for these continued aggressions. The St. Augustine *Herald* editorialized that his policy was already a failure, and Governor Call continued to insist that Florida troops be taken into Federal service. Finally the Legislative Council authorized the raising of twelve companies of volunteers, their officers to be appointed by the governor. If the Federal Government would not have them, then Call was authorized to borrow $500,000 for their pay and equipment. The corps was speedily raised, and Taylor agreed to accept them, provided that only half had horses. The general noted that mounted men were of little value in the hammocks where the Indians were generally found.

Meanwhile, the violence continued. In a short engagement near Fort Mellon, Fanning took eighteen Seminole prisoners. On February 28, Captain Samuel L. Russell, a New Yorker, was shot and killed while traveling in a boat down the Miami River. Near the site of Micanopy, two dispatch riders were wounded. Nothing seemed to dampen the warlike ardor of the remaining Seminole. They were a people who would not yield.

Taylor, however, continued the government's removal policy. On February 25, a further shipment of almost 200 Seminole was dispatched west. Again Taylor made no distinction between Indian and Negro warrior.

Nevertheless, the general's opposition to the use of Florida

Militia and his insistence that their Negro allies be sent with them to the West were causing wide criticism throughout the Territory. The "crackers," the newspapers, even Governor Call himself were all extremely bitter toward the general. Later, Taylor was to write that the Floridians were so antagonistic toward him and the Regulars that cooperation was impossible.

CHAPTER XVII

Macomb's Mission

The major-general commanding in chief
has the satisfaction of announcing to the army
in Florida, to the authorities of the territory,
and to the citizens generally that he has this
day terminated the war with the Seminole Indians . . .

ALEXANDER MACOMB, MAY 18, 1839

By April 1839 the criticism in Florida of General Taylor
had begun to be felt in Washington, and there was talk of
his relief. The matter came to a head in mid-March, when the
War Department announced that its senior officer, Commanding
General of the Army Alexander Macomb, was being sent to the
Territory to see to the protection of its citizens and to end the
War. He was given wide discretion, the only reservation being
that he was not to interfere with Taylor's square system.

Born in Detroit in 1782, Macomb had been living in New
York when, at the age of seventeen, he was commissioned a
cornet of cavalry in the army during the undeclared war with
France. His rise was rapid: he was a lieutenant colonel at the
start of the War of 1812, and on January 24, 1814, at the age of
thirty-two, he became a brigadier general. He was one of the
few authentic heroes to emerge from that war.

195

General Alexander Macomb

Following the War of 1812, Macomb remained on duty, and in the reorganized army of 1821, he was retained as a colonel and chief engineer. On the death of General Jacob Brown in 1828, he became a major general and Commander of the Army.

Tall, with well-proportioned features, he wore his curly black hair somewhat longer than was the custom of his day. Even in late middle age he gave the appearance of youthful vigor. Gregarious and pleasant, he always seemed in a good humor.

In addition, Macomb was a deeply religious man who seldom missed church on Sunday and spent hours studying the Bible. Macomb took considerable pride in being a man of honor, and it was clear there would be no betrayal of a flag of truce while he was in Florida.

Leaving Washington on March 22, 1839, General Macomb and his party arrived at Garey's Ferry early on April 5 and were greeted by a gun salute, Colonel Twiggs and his staff, and the band of the Second Dragoons playing "Hail to the Chief." At breakfast, the party met General Taylor, who had arrived the previous day.

If Taylor had expected to be relieved and returned to the States, he was soon disabused of any such thought. He learned that Macomb's primary reason for being in Florida was to negotiate a peace with the Seminole and bring an expensive war to its end. Nevertheless, Taylor went through the formalities of submitting a request for relief. The people of Florida were so hostile to him and the Regulars that any possibility of communications and cooperation was out of the question, he wrote. Many wanted to continue the conflict, and some were not above inciting the Seminole to continue to fight.

From their first meeting, years before, Taylor had disliked Macomb. He was just not his type of man. Nevertheless, Taylor gave him his full cooperation. Macomb spent his first day being briefed by Taylor, who spared no details and was not at all hesitant to point out the obstacles in the path of Macomb's mission. He told the general that in his opinion nothing could be done with the Indians unless they were permitted to remain in Florida, "and it is a matter of much doubt whether any communication whatever can be had with them."[1] The other officers on the post agreed with Taylor.

The difficulty of inducing any Indians to enter into talks stemmed, of course, from Jesup's refusal to honor a flag of truce. After the experiences of the past, the Seminole were understandably unwilling to accept a white man's word and place themselves within his power. Sam Jones is said to have declared that any messenger sent to him by the whites would be put to death. As Macomb's aide, Lieutenant John Sprague, wrote, "They have been so often deceived and entrapped, that they place no confidence in the most faithful assurances of any white man."

General Taylor, while skeptical, was a soldier and willing to carry out orders. On April 6, 1839, from Garey's Ferry he sent out runners to the Indians inviting them to a conference with General Macomb, to be held at Fort King, starting on May 1.

Escorted by a company of dragoons, General Macomb and his party arrived at Fort King on April 29.

It was not until May 18 that sufficient Indians had arrived in the vicinity of Fort King to make a council possible. Even then the most important Chiefs present, Chitto Tustenuggee and Halleck Tustenuggee, were hardly representative of the Seminole Nation. Nevertheless, Macomb went ahead with the meeting.

To impress the Indians, Macomb convened the council with quite a show. Even General Scott could not have done better. Lieutenant Sprague described the meeting's start:

A Council-Chamber or rather bower was erected within our encampment, covering a circular space of ground, and shut out from the sun by a roof of green bushes, in the center of which was erected a pole to which was attached a white flag. A small room was attached and over the door which communicated with the part occupied by the Indians, the garrison flag was festooned, which very appropriately came just over the General's head. At about 4 P.M. the garrison band of the 7th Infantry Regiment was assembled at Head Quarters together with a company of Dragoons in full uniform as an escort in common time, the band in advance, the General and his staff in full uniform together with all the officers at the post, following, and the Dragoons brought up the rear. Upon each side of the door a soldier was stationed with a white flag, the band passed through and formed on the other side opposite the General's seat while the Dragoons circled around upon the right and left. The officers present took seats upon each side of the General. The Indians were all assembled and looked upon the ceremony with perfect astonishment. The General told them he was glad to see them and they would now "take a smoke" and then [he would] explain to them the object of the council. All who were present, white, black, and yellow, smoked in perfect silence and apparent deep thought for about fifteen minutes, when the general rose, shook hands with all and wished them to listen to his words . . . the words of a friend.[2]

Macomb had been told by all the officers he had met that the War could only be ended by allowing the Seminole to remain in Florida. Exercising the wide authority that he had been given in Washington, he decided that he would terminate the conflict on this basis. He told the hostiles that if they would withdraw south of Pease Creek by July 15, 1839, and thereafter remain within specified boundaries, "until further arrangements could be made," the United States would terminate the conflict. After two days of talks the Indians agreed to the terms. A General Order was issued announcing that hostilities had ceased.

After a second council on May 22, when presents were distributed to the Indians, General Macomb and his staff left Fort King and the next day started their journey back to Washington. They embarked on a steamship at Palatka and, taking only six days for the return trip, were back in the capital city on May 30. General Macomb's report was received with satisfaction. However, Washington officialdom had no intention of allowing the Seminole to remain in Florida, except as a temporary expedient. The Indians who had attended Macomb's council would have been dismayed had they known of Secretary Poinsett's announcement after the general's return. "I am of the opinion," he said, "that the arrangement made by General Macomb will . . . enable me to remove the Indians from the Territory much sooner than can be done by force."

The results of Macomb's mission were praised throughout the country. *The Army and Navy Chronicle* in New York congratulated the general for reaching an agreement to "afford the Army a respite from a toilsome and inglorious campaign." Even the chauvinistic *Charleston Courier* hailed the accomplishments as just and humane. Its editor wrote: "It would be better to leave the slow but sure influence of advancing civilization to relieve Florida of the remainder of her savage inhabitants, than further to prosecute a war, at the cost of millions, in order to expel a handful of Indians from inaccessible hammock and morass."

Even so, the officers stationed in Florida, including Taylor, remained skeptical of the accomplishments of Macomb's mission. Most of the Regulars agreed with Lieutenant Sprague that the Indians had received "inhuman and barbarous treatment . . . from the white settlers . . .," but felt that things had gone too far to end the War by a negotiated peace. However, the settlement had been negotiated by the Commanding General of the Army, and except for conversations with fellow officers, personal letters home, and notations in their diaries, they kept their opinions to themselves.

Not so discreet, however, were the Florida settlers, who reacted to Macomb's peace with indignation. *The Tallahassee Floridian,* in reporting Macomb's agreement, put on its front page at both top and bottom in large type the words: "SHAME, SHAME, SHAME." Throughout the Territory meetings passed resolutions denouncing the "sham peace," and calling for either the migration or the annihilation of the Seminole. Plans were started to raise a fund to pay a bounty of $200 for every Indian scalp. But Sprague's reaction was typical of that of most army officers when he wrote:

> There is not a white man in nor about Florida, except the regular Army, who dares venture out in any numbers in pursuit of the Indians. The Indians may rest in perfect security if two hundred dollars is all that's offered for their scalps.[3]

However, in spite of the Cassandras, for a period a tenuous peace descended on Florida. There were several incidents, but each was susceptible to explanation. The thirty Seminole held in Tampa for transportation west who escaped on June 5 were said to see no reason why they should be forced to emigrate while other Indians remained in Florida. When hostiles murdered the Chaires family on July 17, the marauders were described as renegade Creek.

Several hopeful signs were to be found in the quiet that descended on Florida. Sam Jones, when he learned of the agreement, ordered his people to abide by its terms. Other tribes seemed to be holding themselves aloof, being neither hostile nor friendly to the whites. General Taylor himself began to be optimistic.

Perhaps the War in Florida was really over.

CHAPTER XVIII

Aftermath

> Those who are safe from Indian alarms, in
> distant cities and peaceful lands may indulge in
> gentle strains of humanity and brotherly love,
> were they dwellers in the log cabins of Florida
> they would attune their notes to harsher meas-
> ures.
>
> GOVERNOR ROBERT R. REID, 1839

Macomb had promised the Indians that a post would be established on the Caloosahatchee River within their reservation where they could trade. He left its establishment to Taylor. In July James B. Dallam, an ex-soldier who had found Florida to his liking, was named trader. Lieutenant Colonel William Harney, with a detachment of twenty-six dragoons armed with the new Colt rifles, was ordered to establish the trading post and afford Dallam all necessary protection. The store was built about twenty miles inland from the mouth of the Caloosahatchee, and Harney established his camp nearby.

On July 23, 1839, Harney, who had been shooting wild boar at the mouth of the river, returned in the early evening to his camp. He was tired and, without determining whether guards had been posted, threw himself down to sleep at a distance from his men. During the night he was awakened by gunfire. His detail was under attack by a band of hostiles led by Hospetarke and Chakaika, the so-called Spanish Indians, who previously had taken no part in the War. Surprised and badly outnumbered, they had no opportunity for defensive action. Harney took off sans trousers. As he ran through the woods, the colonel heard footsteps behind him. Without arms, he nevertheless turned and called out, "Come on, you red devils." He was answered in an Irish brogue, "Holy saints, Colonel, is it you?"—but not in time to stop Harney's fist from knocking his pursuer down. The two men found a skiff and made good their escape down the river.

The hostiles captured eighteen men, between $2,000 and $3,000 worth of trade goods, and $1,500 in silver coins. Dallam and his clerk were killed, while fourteen soldiers escaped. Those who were able to get away, without weapons, barely clothed, and without food, lived under indescribable hardship until they reached Tampa.

A giant Negro slave belonging to Dallam, named Sampson, was wounded in the attack but was later able to get away. His report shocked those who had longed for peace. The Seminole did not generally torture their captives. However, the Negro interpreter and another man, after six agonizing hours of torture, were burned to death. Others of the captives were similarly treated.

While the Indians who had wiped out Harney's detail unquestionably knew of the Macomb agreement, they did not consider themselves bound by it. Had Macomb not been so rushed to get back to Washington, had he secured the agreement of a more representative group of Seminole, the attack might not have occurred. That, of course, is hindsight, but what is certain is that Macomb's peace, or truce, as it might better be called, was over. The antagonists were back where they had been in April.

The sparks from the attack on the Caloosahatchee were to

rekindle a fire that would engulf all Florida. Throughout the
Territory, violent death became commonplace. There followed
several brisk engagements between hostiles and whites. Near
Fort Mellon, Lieutenant W. K. Hanson surrounded an Indian
village, captured the inhabitants, and put them on ships bound
for Charleston. Four soldiers were invited to visit Tiger Tail's
encampment, where they were attacked. Only one escaped. Settlers who had returned to their farms following Macomb's announcement were killed and the half-rebuilt cabins burned.

Again the citizens of Florida reacted by blaming Taylor for
the condition of affairs in the Territory. This time he was
charged with leniency and incompetence. Again Governor Call
interjected himself into the picture, criticizing not only Taylor
and his Regulars, but Secretary of War Poinsett as well.

Washington had had enough. On November 29, 1839, Poinsett recommended to President Van Buren that Governor Call
be removed. He wrote that since Call's relief from command of
the Army of the South, the governor's bitter feeling toward
the Regulars had made cooperation between the Territorial
Government and the army impossible. The President agreed,
and the nomination of Judge Robert Raymond Reid as Governor of Florida was sent to the Senate for approval. Call responded by sending to Congress a 6,000-word polemic attacking
both the President and the Secretary of War. He wrote:

> If it be an offense requiring such a penalty, to hold the plans
> and policy pursued by Mr. Poinsett in prosecuting the Florida
> War in contempt, a policy which has desolated the fairest portion
> of this Territory, bankrupt the National Treasury, and covered
> our people with mourning . . . Your Memorialist pleads guilty.
> . . . If the removal from office of your Memorialist was neces-
> sary to sustain the political party of the President in this Territory,
> let this also be assigned as a reason. . . .

In spite of Call's efforts, Reid's nomination was confirmed by the Senate, and he was sworn in as governor. Almost the antithesis of Call, the new executive was an introspective legal scholar who would have been more at home in ivy-covered walls than in the give-and-take of frontier politics. A native of South Carolina, he was an intellectual in the best sense. Although he was a shrewd judge of men, his urbane culture and humanitarian instincts hardly fitted him to be Governor of Florida in 1839.

Meanwhile a series of episodes had accrued that were bizarre even for the Seminole War. Before his dismissal from office, Governor Call had developed a secret weapon—the possibility of importing bloodhounds from Cuba to use in tracking hostiles. The dogs had been successfully employed by the British against the Maroons in Jamaica in 1738, and had brought that eighty-year revolt to an end within a year.

Since General Taylor showed little interest in the idea, on his own initiative Call dispatched Colonel Richard Fitzpatrick to Cuba, where, aided by Colonel Joseph Alzuarde, he purchased thirty-three dogs for $151.72 apiece and hired four handlers.[1] The trip back to Port Leon was a rough one. Having run into foul weather and troubled waters, they landed in Florida with a cargo of seasick hounds.

When word of what was being contemplated became known, the Floridians were delighted. The *Tallahassee Star* exalted, "If these hounds are put into service, we have more confidence in the speedy close of the war than ever before."

The bloodhounds, placed in the custody of Colonel John B. Collins, were taken to Magnolia for acclimation and training. A Negro slave was directed to run a mile in the woods and then climb a tree. The dogs put on the trail were soon able to find him.

Word of the program had reached the North, and criticism of the use of bloodhounds began to trickle into Florida. Governor Reid, in a message to the Legislative Council, defended the use of dogs. He wrote:

> No occasion [has arisen] for testing the usefulness of the dogs brought from Cuba. It is still believed, however, that they may be used with effect; and why should they not be used. If robbers and assassins assail us, may we not defend our property and our lives even with bloodhounds? Shall we look upon our ruined dwellings —upon the mangled bodies of men, women and children, and then meekly say, "the poor Indians have done this—we must be merciful and humane to them—we will not set our dogs upon them—" oh no! that would be more horrible than these butcheries!

Shortly after the dogs arrived in Florida, Governor Reid offered them to Taylor. The general agreed to accept two Cubans and their bloodhounds, and on February 2, the dogs were delivered to Lieutenant George Wood. The next day, an additional six dogs were turned over to R. B. Lanton of the Second Dragoons. The navy also became interested and dispatched Lieutenant John T. McLaughlin in the schooner *Flint* to Cuba to secure the service of several trainers and a supply of dogs.

Back in Washington, the War Department had become concerned over the possible public reaction to the use of the animals. Secretary Poinsett accordingly admonished General Taylor that the use of the bloodhounds ". . . be confined, altogether to tracking down the Indians . . . that they be muzzled when in the field and held with a leash while following the track of the enemy." In no case were the dogs to be allowed to disturb Indian women and children. The execution of this selectivity was left, no doubt, to the discretion of the hounds.

The hounds were taken to Garey's Ferry, where a series of experiments was carried out. An Indian prisoner was released and told to travel four miles and hide in a tree. The dogs went unerringly to the tree where the red man was concealed. Some hostiles were even captured when the bloodhounds were taken on scouting parties. Newspaper accounts called the experiment a great success. The *Jacksonville Advocate* referred to the dogs as "peace hounds."

Governor Reid was encouraged. The Territory of Florida had by now a considerable investment in dogs. Reid sent a bill for the cost of the sixteen hounds that the army had used at this point. He hoped that Taylor would pay the costs of procuring and keeping the dogs. He was shocked when Taylor wrote back that when the bloodhounds ". . . were tendered to me, I informed you in answer that I would make trial of them to ascertain if they would be of service in trailing the Indians. Several experiments have been made with them and the officers having them in charge have reported them of no service whatsoever. Such being the case, I do not feel authorized to order payment for them. . . ."

General Taylor was not just saving the Federal Government the cost of the dogs. They had indeed proven a failure under combat conditions. The numerous lakes, swamps, and streams of Florida had prevented the dogs from following a trail for any great distance. Furthermore, generations of the hounds had been trained in Cuba to follow the scent of Negroes, and many of the animals refused to follow the trail of a Seminole. The experience of the navy was no better. On a scouting patrol, Lieutenant McLaughlin found no Indians, but one of the dogs died of exhaustion.

In the North, however, those opposed to the War made good use of the bloodhound experiment. Congressmen were deluged with letters from their constituents protesting the use of dogs to trail human beings. A flood of petitions on the subject was presented to Congress and duly referred to the Committee on Military Affairs.

The members of the Philadelphian Yearly Meeting of

Lithograph b

. Baillie, 1848

Friends, who were bitterly opposed to the War, but afterwards not at all averse to enjoying its fruits by investing in Florida land, protested such inhuman methods of warfare in a letter to Congress. The correspondent of the *Savannah Georgian,* who had visited Florida, criticized the program in a different tone. From Garey's Ferry, he wrote:

> Eleven of these Florida bloodhounds alias Cuban curs, are now at this post, feasting upon their six pounds of fresh beef each, per day. They have been tried frequently within the last few days with an Indian prisoner *de guerre* at this place, and if they will take his trail, it would be hard to prove it by those who were present. I have no confidence however, in them.
>
> As to their ferocity, it is all humbug—a child may fondle with them. They have been more grossly misrepresented than any set of animals in the world, the army not excepted.

In Congress, Senator Thomas Hart Benton presented a petition opposing the use of bloodhounds, signed, as he said, by the best people of Missouri. Senator Daniel Webster, noting that the protests had not forced the government to disavow the use of bloodhounds, asked for decisive action, "that the public might be disabused."

In the House, Representative George Proffit of Indiana demanded the name of the army officer who had sanctioned the bloodhound plan. Abolitionist Congressman Joshua Giddings of Ohio declared that the dogs had been imported to catch runaway slaves, not to end the War. Former President John Quincy Adams, now a member of the House, in a more humorous mood introduced a resolution asking that:

> The Secretary of War be directed to report to this house, the natural, political, and martial history of the bloodhounds, showing the peculiar fitness of that class of warriors to be the associates of

the gallant army of the United States, specifying the nice dis-
crimination of his scent between the blood of the freeman and the
blood of the slave . . . between the blood of savage Seminoles
and that of the Anglo-Saxon pious Christian. . . . Whether
measures have been taken to secure the employment of this auxil-
iary force, and whether he deems it expedient to extend to the
same bloodhounds and their posterity the benefits of the pension
laws.[2]

The War in Florida ground on. Daily the small detachment
in each of Taylor's squares went out on its patrols, and occasionally it would meet with groups of three or four Indians.
A soldier would be wounded or killed, or perhaps an Indian or
two would be shot or captured. On March 28, 1840, Captain
Gabriel J. Rains of the Seventh Infantry led a patrol of sixteen
men from Fort King. A West Point graduate of 1827, Rains, a
North Carolinian, was an able officer. This time, however, he
was careless and led his men into an ambush. Two men were
killed and a third was wounded. The hostiles numbered almost
a hundred, and Rains saw that he would soon be surrounded.
Leading a charge of a dozen men toward the fort, he was badly
wounded but was nevertheless able to withdraw his detachment.
In reward he received a brevet majority.

Nor was all the violence in Florida confined to Indians and
whites. Florida was still a frontier, and there was often resort to
guns in settling disputes between whites. Sitting down to dinner
one night in the City Hotel in Tallahassee, Colonel Leigh Read,
of Withlacoochee Blockhouse fame, was attacked by Willis Alston,
whose brother Read had killed in a duel. He was shot in the ab-
domen, but recovered, only to be killed later by the same assail-
ant.

Florida was, however, making progress. In spite of the War,
its population in the 1840 census had grown to 54,477 persons, a
growth of almost 20,000. Middle Florida had more than

doubled its inhabitants. It had been necessary for troops to escort the census takers, but the count had been made.

There were other signs of progress in the Territory. Southern College had been founded in St. Augustine. The number of newspapers had doubled in a decade, and every little village seemed to have its own journal. Although transfer between ships was necessary, it was now possible to travel by steamship from Maine to Picolata.

Although the Territorial credit had been strained by the War and Florida had a per-capita debt of almost $140, the Territory seemed in reasonably good economic condition and its bonds were selling at two percent above par on the European market. In Philadelphia and New York its securities were "gobbled up."

There were also stirrings toward statehood in the Territory. In January 1839 a Constitutional Convention had been held at St. Joseph. The document drafted there was submitted to the people and carried by the small edge of 95, out of 4,000 votes cast.

Nevertheless, General Taylor, worn and ill, was tired of the abuse he was receiving. He again submitted a request for recall, and this time, on April 21, 1840, it was granted. He wanted so to get out of the Territory that when his replacement had not arrived three weeks later, he turned over the command on an acting basis to his senior officer, Colonel David E. Twiggs, and left for the North, happy to shake the sands of Florida from his boots.

CHAPTER XIX

Walker Keith Armistead

And this is warfare, glorious, noble, chivalrous warfare.[1]

A DISILLUSIONED LIEUTENANT, 1840

Colonel Twiggs had high hopes that he would be named Commanding General of the Army of the South. The War Department thought differently, picking Brevet Brigadier General Walker Keith Armistead. Twiggs evidently felt that Armistead had pulled strings for the assignment, for thereafter he refused even to shake hands with his commander. Armistead took over on May 5, 1840.

A Virginian, Armistead was said to have been named to West Point from the ranks.[2] A handsome heavy-set man of medium height, with a large head, a cherubic mouth, and curly black hair, he was a punctilious soldier who never deviated from the book. He also seemed to care little for what others might think of him.

In the War of 1812, he served on the Niagara front, rising to the rank of lieutenant colonel. In 1818, he became a full colonel and a chief of engineers. In the reorganized and reduced Army of 1821, he became commanding officer of the Third Artillery. For meritorious service for ten years in one grade, in 1828 he was given a brigadier's brevet. He had previously served in Florida under General Jesup.

Armistead's plan of campaign was not much different from those of his predecessors. He would establish his headquarters at Fort King. Above that point, the Territory would be garrisoned by militia and volunteers, while the Regulars would harass the Seminole to the south. Nine hundred troops, divided into detachments of a hundred men each, would be based at Fort King, from where they could be sent as needed. Particular emphasis would be placed on discovering and destroying the crops that the Indians necessarily grew to sustain themselves. Colonel Twiggs was given command of the zone east of the Suwannee River, while Lieutenant Colonel John Greene was ordered to move up and down the west bank of that river to prevent enemy infiltration to the North. Armistead moved his main supply depot from Garey's Ferry to Palatka and established general hospitals in the Cedar Keys, on the Gulf, and at Picolata.

The general's program was soon put to the test. In late April four families were murdered along the Apalachicola River. Newnansville was attacked, but was saved by a detachment from Fort King. On May 19, Coacooche or Wildcat, with 100 Negro and Indian warriors, hit a detail led by Lieutenant James S. Sanderson, a New Englander who had risen from the ranks, eight miles east of Micanopy. The lieutenant and five of his men were killed. Four days later, only a mile from Fort Weadman on the road from Picolata to St. Augustine, the same group of hostiles ambushed a theatrical troupe traveling in an unescorted wagon.[3] Three of the actors were killed, while three others and the Negro driver escaped. The Seminole were overjoyed to find eighteen trunks of stage costumes. As the warriors were appropriating the finery, another wagon, this one in United States service, approached. In it were three whites and a Negro driver. Two of the whites were killed, but the third white and the driver escaped to Fort Weadman.

In the months that followed Armistead's assumption of command, the Seminole did not have it entirely their own way. A number of the younger officers were willing to disregard army regulations while learning the rudiments of guerrilla warfare. One such officer was Captain Benjamin L. E. Bonneville, a native Frenchman and a graduate of the class of 1815 at West Point. In June, with a detachment of 100 men, he explored the Big Swamp. Although only fifteen miles from Fort King, it had not been seriously searched since the start of the War, and the Seminole considered themselves entirely safe within its wild fastness. Surprising a large group of Seminole during the ceremony of a Green Corn Dance, Bonneville's men killed a number of the Indians. The soldiers suffered one fatality.

Another young firebrand was a Marylander, Lieutenant Bennett Riley. On June 2, 1840, he attacked and destroyed an important Indian stronghold at Chocachatti. For his courage that day, he was made a brevet colonel.

And of course there was the bullheaded Lieutenant Colonel "Bill" Harney, still smarting from his carelessness and the subsequent defeat of his detail on the Caloosahatchee while guarding Macomb's trading post. The memory of having to run in his shorts rankled like a cancerous sore, and he determined to be even more crafty than his savage foes. Armistead's request that Harney disguise his men as Indians was refused as not being according to the book, but when distant from Fort King, Harney employed the ruse. With a detachment of dragoons, he destroyed hundreds of acres of Seminole crops in areas previously thought inaccessible.

Although General Armistead had no high regard for citizen-soldiers, he made use of them. Accordingly, in July he called on Governor Reid for 1,500 men. This was humiliating, for he

Lithograph l

ames & Gray

didn't like Reid any better than Jesup had liked Call, but the additional troops were necessary to garrison the area above Fort King.

At dawn on August 7, 1840, there occurred far to the south at Indian Key a tragedy that was to stir the nation. Doctor Henry Perrine, a New York physician and a distinguished botanist, while serving at Campeachy from 1827 until 1838 as American Consul, determined to devote the remainder of his life to the introduction and acclimation of "useful tropical plants in semi-tropical Florida." His decision was acclaimed by a number of scientists and by the Senate Committee on Agriculture. On July 7, 1838, Congress granted Doctor Perrine and his associates a township of land in South Florida. Concluding that it would be unsafe to go on his land, Perrine determined to start his experiments at Captain Housman's Indian Key Village. He went there with his family in December 1838. The life must have been lonely for them, for the doctor, an extremely straitlaced man, refused to allow his family to have any social intercourse with Housman or the woman the captain called his wife. He also refused to allow his daughters to meet any of the many young navy and army officers at the key. Perrine happily carried on his experiments for a period of twenty months.

Housman's militia had been disbanded in 1838. The revenue cutter stationed at Indian Key was on patrol. The village was completely undefended when a band of the Spanish Indians, in seventeen canoes, struck; they were led by Chakaika, who had humbled Colonel Harney. Thirteen of the villagers, including the doctor, were killed. Perrine's family, after hiding in a cellar of their burning home, escaped to Tea Table Key, the base of a naval detachment. There they found most of the other survivors.[4]

When the refugees from Indian Key began straggling in, there were only the surgeon and twelve patients at Tea Table. Nevertheless, a midshipman, Murray, who was himself ill,

loaded a cannon and five of the less sick gobs aboard a small boat
and set out for Indian Key. As they approached the shore and
the Indians opened fire, the midshipman let go with his cannon.
It recoiled overboard, almost swamping the boat. Unfortunately
the Indians had found Housman's six-pounder, and, having
loaded it with musket balls, they fired at the boat. Murray could
do nothing but withdraw, and the warriors were left to continue
their looting.

As a result of the Indian Key Massacre and Doctor Perrine's
death, more Florida Militia were inducted into Federal service
and the Eighth Infantry was sent to Florida. There were now in
the Army of the South ten companies of the Second Dragoons
based at Fort Heilman, nine companies of the Third Artillery at
St. Augustine, the First, Second, and Eighth Infantry at Fort
King, the Third and Sixth Infantry at Fort Brooke and the
Seventh at Micanopy.

General Armistead, with a formidable force behind him,
next turned to diplomacy. A council was set up in early November 1840 at Fort King, with Tiger Tail, who was a Tallahassee,
and Halleck Tustenuggee, a Mikasukim.

Tiger Tail—over six feet tall, dark, and well proportioned,
with a craggy face and a large nose and mouth—was perhaps the
most civilized of all Seminole. As a boy he had been raised in
the village of his father on the site of what later became the
town of Tallahassee. Not far away on the Cauculla River was
the home of Robert Gamble. The young Indian became a friend
of the Gambles and soon was in their home as much as in his
own. Gamble was a banker and a cultured gentleman, and the
boy soon learned the ways of the whites and to speak English
fluently. He adopted many of their customs and was poised and
at home in their company. He was extremely intelligent.

Halleck Tustenuggee hated all whites, but his customary
Indian courtesy belied this. Whites who knew him, however,

said that underneath he was cold and without pity. He was said to have killed his own sister when she favored compromise with the whites.

As the time for the council approached, General Armistead directed that commanders in the field should avoid all hostile operations for the present. The order was resented, but the usual patrol actions were canceled.

At the conference, which started on November 10, 1840, Armistead's only innovation was an attempt at bribery. He offered the two Chiefs $5,000 each if they would bring in their bands for shipment west. The Indians told the general they would like two weeks to think it over. Before that time had elapsed, they had fled.

It was about this time that another idea, dreamed up in the War Department in Washington, was tried. A delegation of twelve Seminole was brought from Fort Gibson to persuade the Florida Indians to join them in the West. The effort was a failure, for not one red man was persuaded to migrate. The War was again resumed.

Reverberations from the killing of Doctor Perrine were still to be heard, and Colonel Harney saw in them an opportunity to revenge his humiliation on the Caloosahatchee. In late November he persuaded General Armistead to allow him to go after Chakaika. On December 4, he set out from Fort Dallas* with a force of ninety men in sixteen canoes. The men from the Second Dragoons and Third Artillery, armed with Colt rifles, were guided by a Negro named John. Traveling through what seemed, as a soldier wrote, ". . . a vast sea, filled with grass and green trees"[5] and without distinguishing landmarks, the detachment threaded its way through the Everglades. The force overtook and captured several parties of Indians. Harney hanged the warriors on the spot and kept the women and chil-

---

* Located in what is now downtown Miami.

dren as prisoners. When John once appeared to be lost, Harney threatened his captured squaws. If they would not guide him, he would hang their children. On their refusal, however, he backed down.

Chakaika and his Spanish Seminole considered their remote Everglade redoubt to be impossible for the whites to discover. No guards had been posted, and the huge Chief was chopping wood when Harney and his men arrived at the Indian camp a few hours after dawn. The Seminole were taken by surprise. Chakaika had started to surrender when he was shot and killed. Most of the other warriors, however, were able to escape. Three were captured. Harney had two of them hanged in the presence of their wives and children. The third he kept for a guide. Chakaika's body was also strung up. Four Indians had been killed in action, and five had been hanged. The soldiers with their prisoners then retraced their steps to Fort Dallas. The colonel had had his revenge.

Harney was acclaimed by all Florida. The Legislative Council of the Territory not only voted him a resolution of thanks, but awarded him a handsomely engraved sword.

Although the policy of constantly sending out patrols from the many posts in the Territory was having its effect, and the Seminole were feeling the attrition, the Mikasukis launched a fresh offensive in late December. On the 28th, led by Halleck Tustenuggee, they ambushed a detail of thirteen men of the Seventh Infantry, all mounted, escorting an officer's wife from Fort Micanopy to Fort Wacahoota. The first volley killed Mrs. Alexander Montgomery, Second Lieutenant Walter Sherwood, and three enlisted men. Pursuers from Fort Micanopy failed to find the hostiles.

The Seminole were not so successful when Halleck tried to lure Lieutenant William Alburtis into a trap on the Oklawaha River. Alburtis, a Virginian and an able officer, was able to work his troops into a position behind the Indians and establish a counter-ambush. A number of the Seminole were killed, and the rest fled. Halleck Tustenuggee's band later attacked a supply train in the same area, but a white counter-charge soon scattered the enemy, who again fled.

Refusing to recognize a distinction between Indians and their Negro allies, Armistead had by March over 300 Indians and Negroes at Tampa awaiting shipment west. Most had been taken prisoner by the daily patrols, but others were there thanks to the general's resorting to bribery. He had been given $25,000 for this purpose by the War Department, but he asked for another $30,000. For $5,000, he was able to induce Coosa Tustenuggee, a Mikasuki, and his band of sixty to surrender. Most of the Chiefs did not take the bait. They would come in and talk, but, after sampling Armistead's whiskey, food, and presents, would never quite agree. Even Coacoochee, or Wildcat, dressed as Hamlet in a costume looted from the theatrical troupe, escorted by followers similarly arrayed in theatrical finery, entered into negotiations at Fort Cummings in March. The officers present at the parley long remembered the Chief's words:

> The whites . . . dealt unjustly by me. I came to them, they deceived me; the land I was upon I loved, my body is made of its sands; the Great Spirit gave me legs to walk over it; hands to aid myself; eyes to see its ponds, rivers, forests, and game; then a head with which I think. The sun, which is warm and bright as my feelings are now, shines to warm us and bring forth our crops, and the moon brings back the spirit of our warriors, our fathers, wives, and children. The white man comes; he grows pale and sick, why cannot we live here in peace? I have said I am the enemy to the white man. I could live in peace with him, but they first steal our cattle and horses, cheat us, and take our lands. The white men are as thick as the leaves in the hammocks; they come upon us thicker every year. They may shoot us, drive our women and children night and day; they may chain our hands and feet, but the red man's heart will be always free.[6]

Although he had failed to induce Wildcat to give up, General Armistead felt that his accomplishments had been considerable. Under his leadership 450 Indians and Negroes had been sent west, and in mid-March 235 were waiting for ships at Tampa. He was nevertheless, like all of his predecessors, tired and fed up with Florida, and he asked the War Department for relief. On May 31, 1841, his request was granted.

The conflict was now in its sixth year, and opposition not only to its conduct but to the War itself had steadily grown both in the Congress and in the country. The War had not only contributed to the growth of the abolitionist movement, but had become intermixed with the entire question of slavery. In 1836 the House of Representatives forbade the discussion of slavery petitions on its floor. In February 1841, when several members objected to the payment of bribes to the Seminole Chiefs, Representative Joshua Giddings of Ohio seized the opportunity for an attack on the institution of slavery. Attempts were made to rule him out of order, but he maintained the floor, charging that Georgia, with the help of the entire South, had induced the United States to use its army on a slave-catching expedition and that such use was contrary to the Constitution. Thereafter, throughout the nation, the Seminole War could not be discussed without the subject of slavery being introduced.

CHAPTER XX

William Jenkins Worth

And yet 'tis not an endless War
As facts will plainly show
Having been ended forty times
In twenty months or so.

ARMY SONG, 1841[1]

Colonel William Jenkins Worth, who relieved General Armistead on May 31, 1841, was a man of great physical and mental energy. He was one of the ablest of those who commanded the Army of the South.

Born a Quaker in 1794, he became a first lieutenant in 1813 during the War of 1812. Of medium height, he gave the appearance of great physical strength and was an ardent believer in the strenuous life. In the field he was both confident and decisive, but he was unfortunately inclined, like several of his predecessors, to put his foot in his mouth. He was also vain, self-centered, and given to boasting.

In the War of 1812 Worth had received a brevet promotion following both the battles of Chippewa and Niagara. At Lundy's Lane on June 25, 1814, he took a fragment of grape-shot in the loin; he was permanently lame thereafter.

224

General William J. Worth

As did his predecessors, Worth had preconceived ideas on how the War could be won. The Seminole War was never to be quite the same again after Worth assumed command. He would first rid the Territory of Indians between the Withlacoochee and the white settlements, driving them to the south. Then, with his Regulars divided into small detachments fighting as guerrillas, he would constantly harass the Seminole bands. Driving his men mercilessly, he would keep them in the field all four seasons of the year.

Having no greater regard for volunteers than did the other army officers, Worth determined to place his chief reliance on Regulars. This was not always easy. When, shortly after taking command, he discharged four companies of Georgia Militia, the protests could be heard as far as Washington. The Governor of Georgia cried, "They [the militiamen] are now to be coolly turned off; the protection of their homes confided to strangers, with whom they hold not one feeling in common." Evidence was also submitted to the Secretary of War that Regular troops had stolen a barrel of whiskey, killed hogs and cattle, beaten one man, and killed another. Later, it developed that the latter, a drunken civilian, had been shot in self-defense. Except for moving the unit involved, Worth ignored the charges.

Worth also brought additional local civilian wrath down on his head by his efforts to economize. The War was now costing over $92,000 a month, and when the colonel set about reducing civilian employees, the cries of anguish resounded to heaven. As Lieutenant John T. Sprague wrote,

> . . . A discharge from public employment, under any circumstances of necessity or economy was by a large number considered a grievous wrong. The military, from the commander down, were considered aggressors upon the rights and liberty of the civilian.[2]

Colonel Worth also set in action a program of white resettlement. Settlers were not only encouraged to return to their lands by the promise of army help, but Lieutenant Marsena R. Patrick, a native New Yorker and West Point graduate, was appointed to encourage the resettlement. The settlers were given army rations, and by early 1842 there were 652 men, women, children, and slaves living in twelve resettlement villages.

At the same time, Colonel Worth pursued the Indians with a vigor Florida had not known. Larger commands were broken down into units of twenty men plus a troop of dragoons. Their officers were directed to "keep the men in constant motion, . . . [and] tax their strength to the utmost." Soldiers were offered a reward of a hundred dollars for every warrior captured or killed. It was rough on the troops, and by July 1841 there were over 2,400 men on the sick list. The policy seemed, however, to be paying off, and every week there were reports of warriors killed or captured.

Nevertheless, the Seminole depredations and murders and the complaints of the Floridians continued. Here and there a settler and his family would be taken unawares and ruthlessly killed. Lone travelers on roads heretofore thought safe were ambushed and slain. The Territorials blamed it on the army, who, they insisted, had still not learned Indian warfare. Militia could win the war, they said, not the rigid popinjays that the Regulars called soldiers.

The rest of the country was no happier with the performance of the army than were the residents of Florida, although for a different reason. The extended Florida conflict had become extremely unpopular. Already the cost of the War was approaching the astronomical sum of $40,000,000 and the army mortality rate had gone well beyond 1,400 men—a death rate of fourteen percent. President Martin Van Buren's defeat in 1840 and the election of the Whig candidate General William Henry Harrison, the hero of Tippecanoe, were generally ascribed to the failure of the former to bring "Jackson's War" to a conclusion. Harrison, in his short month's tenure in the presidency, did not have an opportunity to conclude the conflict, but his successor, Vice President John Tyler, although a Democrat, finally ended the War. Before his death, Harrison did, however, dismiss Governor Reid and bring Richard K. Call, now a Whig, back to the office.

Nor was the Administration alone in its determination to finish the fighting. Colonel William Jenkins Worth decided that he would bring an end to the War, no matter what means were necessary. Among the policies that he employed was the use of the same sort of treachery that had previously stained General Jesup's name.

On May 1, 1841, Lieutenant William Tecumseh Sherman had been sent out by Brevet Lieutenant Colonel Thomas Childs to escort Coacoochee to Fort Pierce to discuss plans for bringing his people in for migration. Sherman, a perceptive and able young 1840 West Point graduate, took no chances. He saw that Coacoochee and his small group of warriors were disarmed before starting back toward the fort. He did, however, stop to allow the Chief to bathe himself in a pool and to don his best finery for a ceremonial entrance into Fort Pierce.

During the council that followed, Colonel Childs agreed that Coacoochee could have thirty days to prepare his tribe for migration. Childs, of the First Artillery, was also a Military Academy graduate, having entered the army in 1814 as a 3rd lieutenant. He had seen considerable service during the Seminole War and was regarded as an able officer. By June 4 he had become convinced that Coacoochee had no intention of keeping his agreement. He accordingly had the Seminole Chief and fifteen tribesmen seized and made prisoners.

Later, Lieutenant Colonel William Gates of the Third Artillery, a crusty old New England-bred West Pointer who had been in the army since 1806, ordered that Coacoochee and his warriors be slapped into irons and shipped to New Orleans. Worth, who had hoped to make use of the Chief in order to bring in others, countermanded the order and had the group brought to Tampa. There the colonel bluntly told the warriors that if the entire tribe did not come in, the sixteen would be hanged. With the added incentive, if added incentive was needed, of a promise of $8,000 if he was successful, Coacoochee set about sending out emissaries to his people. Almost all of his tribe came to Tampa and were made prisoners.

Thereafter Worth made use of Coacoochee to induce Hospetarke to attend a council aboard a ship in the harbor. The ruse was again successful: the flag of truce was violated, and the old Chief and his party were seized. On October 12, 1841, over 200 Indians were shipped west.

In mid-October another attempt was made to induce migration by bringing to Florida a small delegation of Chiefs who had previously been sent west. The emissaries, headed by Alligator, were able to persuade Tiger Tail and his brother Nethlockemathla and their tribesmen to turn themselves in at Fort Brooke. Altogether, fifty-two men and 110 women and children arrived at Tampa on October 19, 1841.

In spite of these successes, Worth gave no sign of relenting on pushing his troops to the utmost. The commanders of the military districts to the north were told to keep two-fifths of their troops always in the field. "Find the enemy, capture or exterminate," was the order governing commanders in their operations.[3]

Colonel Worth, in his effort to bring the War to a conclusion, was fortunate in having the wholehearted cooperation of the naval forces. The commander of the flotilla in Florida waters, Lieutenant John T. McLaughlin, was a vigorous, imaginative young man who sincerely believed in good army–navy relations. McLaughlin, the son of a Baltimore tailor, had been

severely wounded on February 8 at Lake Monroe while serving in Florida in a subordinate capacity in 1837. After a con-
valescence of some nineteen months, he volunteered for a
return to combat and was given command of all naval units in
the Territory and adjacent waters. His force included seven vessels, 140 canoes, and a miscellaneous assortment of small boats.
Serving under him were fifty officers, 285 sailors, and, since
Henderson had returned to his duties in Washington, the one
hundred marines he had left behind. Like Worth, McLaughlin
pushed his men to the limits of their endurance. The naval
squadron in Florida was not deactivated until August 3, 1842.

Even before Worth assumed command, McLaughlin, setting out in December 1840, led a flotilla of sailor-manned dug-
outs through the Everglades, from the Gulf of Mexico to the
Atlantic. They were the first white men to span the Everglades.

Now, in the fall of 1841, the lieutenant was ordered by
Worth to repeat his feat. With a command composed of sol-
diers, sailors, and marines, the force set out in canoes from Punta
Rossa, went up the Caloosahatchee River, crossed Lake Okee-
chobee, and after a trek over land finally reached the Atlantic at
Fort Lauderdale.

The expedition was gone for two months, the men suffering
indescribable hardships. A number collapsed and died. The results were minimal: only a handful of Indians were killed or
captured.

Not all of the operations were fruitless, however. At one
point two Seminole were discovered in the vicinity of Fort Lauderdale. On another occasion, six warriors were killed, and sixty
captured.

Major Thomas Childs' command discovered hundreds of
acres of cultivated fields along the Indian River. They were so
extensive that eighty men were occupied for two days in their
destruction.

Nor were the Seminole entirely idle. Central and North

Florida continued to be drenched in blood. On December 20, 1841, Halleck Tustenuggee, leading fifteen warriors, attacked the village of Mandarin, on the east bank of the Indian River, thirty-five miles north of St. Augustine. Four persons were murdered, several buildings were burned, and as much loot as possible was carried off. The Indians had the impudence to occupy the town overnight, and the cries of indignation of the Floridians grew louder. Colonel Worth himself hurried north to take charge.

Hundreds of troops were put in the field, and the going was rough. Some of the soldiers were said to have spent two-thirds of their time slogging through Florida waters. It was not, however, until January 25, 1842, that contact was made with Halleck's band. They were located by a detachment of over 100 men led by Major Joseph Plympton of the Second Infantry. A Yankee who had received a direct commission during the War of 1812, Plympton found the enemy camped in a hammock near Dunn's Lake about twenty-five miles south of St. Augustine. When discovered, the Indians hastily withdrew to cover, and it took over an hour of heated battle before they were dislodged. In the pursuit that followed, no hostiles were taken, and if there were any Seminole fatalities, this was not reported. Thereafter the search for Halleck and his band continued, but without result.

In the South, Major William G. Belknap, a tough old New York veteran of both the War of 1812 and Indian fighting in the West, made contact on December 20 with a band led by Bowlegs. There were a few Seminole casualties and several prisoners taken, but most of the warriors were successful in eluding pursuit.

Nevertheless, as 1842 dawned, the Seminole were at their lowest point. It was estimated that only about 300 hostiles remained in Florida, and of these only about 112 braves remained on the warpath. Scattered in small detachments of never more than twenty men, they still constituted a deadly nuisance. Concluding that the balance of the hostiles could not be brought in by force, Worth, after shipping west about 230 Seminole, including a few Negroes, recommended to the War Department that the rest of the Indians be allowed to remain in Florida. Army strength in the Territory could be reduced, and the troops remaining would be used exclusively to protect settlements. While seriously considered by Washington, the proposal was eventually rejected. The proposition did, however, bring down on the colonel the rage of the citizens of Florida. It was obvious that they would not be satisfied as long as one Indian remained alive on Territorial soil. The conflict continued.

The last major battle of the War took place near Lake Ahapopka, about twenty miles southwest of Fort Mellon, where the troops made contact with Halleck and a band of about forty warriors on April 19, 1842. The Seminole were dug in on a small hammock surrounded by water. They had cleared a field of fire and erected a breastwork. Opposing them were 400 troops from the Second, Fourth, and Eighth Infantries and a detachment of dragoons led by Colonel Worth himself. The infantry, knee-deep in mud and stinking vegetation, made a frontal attack on the Indian position while the colonel dispatched the dragoons against the enemy rear. As in the past, the hostiles simply seemed to evaporate, and for his trouble Worth was left with a quantity of Indian gear and provisions, and with one soldier killed and four wounded.

The Battle of Lake Ahapopka had its effect, however, and on April 29, under a flag of truce, Halleck came into the army camp at Warm Springs for a parley. With him were two of his wives and two children. Worth persuaded the Chief to accompany him to Fort King. Before leaving, the colonel directed Colonel Garland to wait three days and then seize the remainder of the Indians. Garland, a Virginian commissioned in 1812, invited the Seminole to a dinner, where he plied the red men with

232

whiskey. When they were sufficiently inebriated, they were surrounded and taken prisoner. Lieutenant Sprague, writing of
Halleck, had this to say:

> Whatever sins may be laid to . . . this Indian chieftain, or
> however diabolical the instinct of his nature, his land was dearer
> to him than life. For if he had fought boldly and unceasingly; and
> had adopted the alternative of the feeble, treachery, and against
> the strong, to maintain his inheritance. Confidence in himself and
> those within his influence, allowed no question of policy, expe-
> diency, or necessity, to alter his resolution, or to restrain him from
> preditory [sic] and cruel acts upon the defenceless and unoffend-
> ing. If this trait in the savage be patriotism, Halleck Tustenug-
> gee's name should stand eternally side by side with the most distin-
> guished of mankind.[4]

Back in early February, Colonel Worth had shipped 280
Seminole west, of whom sixty-eight had been warriors. In July
Halleck's band of forty men and eighty women started the journey. There were thus probably less than a hundred warriors left
in the Territory.

With the War tapering off, Congress did not wait for the
cessation of hostilities to cut military expenditures. During the
conflict the army had not enhanced either its prestige or its
popularity, and it was fair game for the politicians. Although the
Democrats had traditionally distrusted a standing army, the arguments transcended party lines. Those who insisted that the
nation's primary reliance should be on militia and the navy and
that the army should be cut at least to its pre-Seminole strength
of 7,200 officers and men were mostly from the South, but were
joined by a scattering of Northerners, including the redoubtable
John Quincy Adams of Massachusetts.

And again there were cries for the abolition of the Military
Academy at West Point. The anti-military forces were opposed

by a group, primarily from the Middle Atlantic and border states, who argued that the nation could and should support an army of 10,000.

In August 1842 a compromise was reached. In the interest of economy the Second Dragoons were converted into a less expensive rifle regiment and the size of companies was reduced from fifty to forty-two men. The more popular navy, which had extracted what little glamour the Seminole War afforded, saw its appropriation increased.

In August the Armed Occupations Act for Florida was passed. It provided that the head of a family might select and settle on 160 acres of land in the area in Florida three miles north of Palatka and ten miles south of Newnansville. Under its provisions the land selected could not be within two miles of a military post and the patentee was required to erect a cabin, clear five acres, and live on the land for five years. Under the act, which had a lifespan of only a year, 1,317 patents were issued for a total of 210,000 acres.

Meanwhile dislike of the War continued to increase throughout the country. No longer was the conflict opposed by the Whigs alone. More and more Democrats reversed their original positions. It was too much for President Tyler, and on May 10, 1842, the new Secretary of War, John C. Spencer, informed General Scott, who had become Commanding General of the Army on Macomb's death in June 1841, that the Administration wanted an immediate end to hostilities. The implementation and exact date were left to the field commander. Worth was thus authorized to end the fighting, even though all Seminole might not have been sent west.

On the assurance of the Surgeon General that it was the most healthy spot in Florida, Colonel Worth had established his headquarters in the Cedar Keys, and from there he wrote the Adjutant General on June 14:

As yet I have used the authority conferred by the President, in a limited degree, still cherishing the hope that by management, all [the Seminole] may be induced to emigrate; failing in that, I shall unhesitatingly go to the full extent, as the only means of pacifying the Country, and assign them, temporarily, planting and hunting grounds, but far south of any settlements that now are, or like to be for centuries.[5]

Word had reached the Seminole that they could live in peace and still remain in Florida. In spite of Colonel Worth's treatment of Coacoochee and Halleck, a number of the Chiefs and sub-Chiefs arrived at the Cedar Keys headquarters for talks. Fuse Hadjo and Nocosemathla were there on August 5, and Tiger Tail on the 9th. They were told that each warrior who would agree to go west would be given a rifle and ammunition, as well as money and one year's ration. Otherwise, they could live in peace on the same reservation that General Macomb had outlined in 1839, which was to run from the mouth of Pease Creek along its left bank to the fork and thence along its south branch to Lake Istakpoga; from there, down the eastern side of the lake to the creek that emptied into the Kissimmee; thence down the left bank to Lake Okeechobee; and then south through the lake and the Everglades to the Shark River and the Gulf of Mexico. Few of those who conferred with Colonel Worth voted in favor of migration.

Although there had been a few killings of both settlers and Seminole, and a few ships had been lured to their destruction by hostiles in the vicinity of Indian Key, there had been no major fighting for several months.

On August 14, Colonel Worth, by General Order, declared the War at an end. This was followed by his asking for a ninety-day leave. The War Department not only granted his request but gave him a brevet promotion to brigadier general.

Leaving the Territory, Worth turned over the temporary

command to his senior officer, Colonel Josiah H. Vose of the
Fourth Infantry. Vose, born in Massachusetts, had entered the
army as a captain in 1812. He was not only a man of high
principle, but was afraid of no one—not even the War Department. He was put to the test less than a month after he assumed
command in Florida.

Following Worth's departure, several settlers were killed
by Indians in Middle Florida. As usual, a hue and cry arose
from the citizens of the Territory. The Floridians were not
happy about the decision that any Seminole might remain or
about Worth's proclamation that the War had ended. They
blamed the settlers' deaths on the War Department and an in-
competent Regular army. Their insistence that no Indians remain on the soil of Florida was, they felt, entirely justified. The
Administration finally weakened, and on September 12, 1842,
Vose was directed by the War Department to take the field.

Colonel Vose, like most of his contemporaries, was of the
opinion that the troubles in Florida could not be attributed to
the Seminole alone. That there existed ". . . a spirit of implacable resentment towards the Indians in the vagabond class of the
citizens of this territory." The colonel accordingly determined
to ignore the Secretary of War's direction. The Seminole, he
wrote:

> . . . have so far fulfilled, though slowly, every promise they
> have made and it was with no less astonishment than mortification
> that I suddenly found myself instructed . . . to forfeit every
> pledge I had made to the Indians and pursue a course which in
> the present state of affairs would in my opinion not only disperse
> those assembled, under the proclamation for peace, but incite the
> entire Indian population to acts of retaliation and revenge, in-
> evitably tending to reproduce a state of War. After much reflec-
> tion upon the subject, I have determined, in view of all the
> circumstances which surround me, and under the most unpreju-
> diced conviction that it will be for the good of the country, to
> suspend the execution of the Secretary's instructions. . . .[6]

236

It was a courageous act, and Secretary Spencer accepted Vose's judgment, suspending execution of the order.

War Department orders were not the only vexations to plague Colonel Vose during his three months' tenure as Commander of the Army of the South. Army morale was at a low point. There were countless requests from his officers for transfer out of Florida. Resignations of company-grade officers were daily received and forwarded to Washington. A West Point graduate and native of Georgia, Captain Nathaniel W. Hunter of the Second Dragoons, was charged with circulating an anti-War petition. Among enlisted men, the desertion rate soared ominously.

Finally, as if to cap the colonel's woes, on October 4 a devastating hurricane struck the Cedar Keys, and the damage was so extensive that army headquarters had to be evacuated.[7] When General Worth returned on November 1, Colonel Vose requested an immediate transfer out of the Territory.

General Worth, after his return, continued to parley with Tiger Tail. When no final conclusions were reached and it became apparent that the Chief would neither go west nor remove to the reservation, the general ordered that he and his band should be taken by force. Lieutenant Thomas Jordan, a Virginian only two years out from the Military Academy, was dispatched with a detachment of twenty men to bring the Indian in. He found him in his camp about nine miles from the Cedar Keys. The old Chief, who was ill, was ". . . in the midst of a scrub stretched on a bear skin before a small fire."[8] The lieutenant surrounded the camp, taking Tiger Tail and his band of six men and thirteen women and children prisoner. Too sick to walk, the old Indian had to be carried to the Cedar Keys by litter. Later, from Seahorse Key, he and his followers were shipped to New Orleans, where he died.[9]

Only Halpatter, Chitto Hadjo, and Cotsa Fixicochopca now remained at large outside of the reservations. General Worth ac-

237

cordingly offered a reward of $300 for the capture of each of these Chiefs and $100 for each of their warriors. There were no takers. He also shipped west the remainder of the Indian prisoners in his hands.

The general estimated that sixty-two Seminole and ten hostile Creek warriors now remained in Florida. Together with women and children, the Indians in the Territory numbered not over 300. Bowlegs was their acknowledged Chief, with Ossinawa, Otul Kethlocko, and Halpatter Tustenuggee as sub-Chiefs.

The Seminole War did not come to a grinding halt. There was no treaty of peace. The Indians remaining in Florida gradually withdrew into the fastness of the Everglades.

Epilogue

> Ignorance must give way to the restless, ungovernable, and onward course of civilization: yet a nation cannot, disguise it as we may, shake off the responsibility and remorse which will, in all future time, be identified with the fate of the red man.
>
> John T. Sprague, 1848

Army morale during the last years of the Seminole War and following its conclusion was lower than it had ever been in the nation's history. The Regular Army had lost 1,466 men, many of them in Florida. Of about 600 commissioned officers in the army at the start of the War in 1835, sixty-four died during the conflict and many times that number resigned.

Only those officers who were seriously interested in a military career—who wanted to be soldiers—remained in the army. Having served and learned in combat, under conditions as hard as they could ever know, the officers who continued on duty went on to participate, many of them with great distinction, in the Mexican War, the Civil War, and against the Indians on the plains. Florida was the training ground for these conflicts.

The navy, marines and the Revenue Cutter Service emerged from the Seminole War with their prestige enhanced. They had

239

extracted from the conflict what little glory there was. To the American public, their dashing to the rescue of beleaguered towns and forts and the expeditions their officers led in canoes through swamps and rivers had been glamorous. Sixty-nine sailors died in the conflicts.

Cooperation among the services in the Seminole War was probably greater than in any other American conflict. Combined operations actually became, for once in our history, a reality.

While no charges of waste were ever leveled at the army during the Seminole War, its record was hardly one of which its leaders could be proud. A comparative handful of "savages" had fought them to a draw for seven years. If the purpose of the Seminole War had been the complete removal of the Indians from Florida, the army had failed.

Service in Florida had also exposed the military to illness and disease. Between June 28, 1841, and February 28, 1842, 15,794 sick calls were registered—about two for every man in service. And in addition to the deaths, 117 men were seriously disabled.

Estimates of the cost of the Seminole War have run as high as $40,000,000, which was a colossal expenditure for the young republic in 1842. When one considers that only fourteen years before the start of the War, the United States paid Spain only $5,000,000 for the whole of Florida, it is possible to arrive at some conception of the immense dollar cost of the Seminole conflict.

The Seminole War caused division in the nation—a division that a century would not entirely eradicate.

The slaveholders of the South knew that the institution of slavery could not exist while there existed a free enclave into which a fugitive Negro could flee. The Seminole, the Southerners insisted, should be required to take the path previously followed by the Creek, and remove to the West. It is almost certain that the Seminole would reluctantly have agreed to migrate, had they not been required to abandon their vassals and allies, the Negroes. But theirs was a loyalty that has seldom if ever been given by one race to another, and because of it they risked the very existence of the Seminole Nation.

The Seminole War was fought at a great distance from our population center. Communications were often delayed. It took much time to reach the theatre of operation in 1835. Our army seemed unable to grasp the principles of guerrilla warfare. In addition, Washington felt most qualified to determine tactical strategy, thereby controlling the every action of the commanders in the actual field of combat.

Perhaps most important was the attitude of the country toward the War. A democracy cannot fight a prolonged war when there is little glory and few victories. Our country's general reaction to the start of the conflict can be expressed in one word: apathy. In 1835 a mere handful in the Congress opposed the Florida conflict as a war of aggression—as a war in defense of slavery. As the War continued, as the cost in dollars and men soared, more and more of those who had led us down the primrose path reversed their positions. When the War ended, few of our political leaders would admit that they had once supported the conflict.

Harried, tired, and worn, the remnant of the Seminole that withdrew into the fastness of the Everglades could take pride. They had bravely fought for their land and had given the national policy of Indian removal to the far West its firmest opposition.

For decades the small band of Seminole who remained in Florida was rarely seen by white men. By the 1850s and 1860s their numbers had shrunk to below a hundred.

Today they are less than 2,000.

Chapter Notes

(The Florida Historical Quarterly is listed herein as FHQ.)

CHAPTER I

1. See Fry, James Barnet, *The History and Legal Effects of Brevets in the Armies of Great Britain and the United States*, D. Van Nostrand, New York: 1877.

2. Donaldson, Thomas, "The George Catlin Indian Gallery in the U.S. National Museum" (Catlin's Notes), *Annual Report of the Regents of the Smithsonian Institution*, Government Printing Office, Washington, D.C.: 1885, p. 217.

3. Boyd, Mark F., "Asi-Yaholo or Osceola," FHQ, Vol. XXXIII, Nos. 3 and 4, January–April 1955, p. 249.

4. Motte, Jacob Rhett, *Journey into Wilderness*, University of Florida Press, Gainesville, Florida: 1953, p. 141.

5. Ibid., p. 140.

6. Jarvis, Nathan S., "An Army Surgeon's Notes on Frontier Service," *Journal of the Military Service Institution of the United States*, September–October 1906, p. 277.

7. Smith, W. W., *Sketch of the Seminole War*, D. J. Dowling, Charleston, South Carolina: 1836, p. 5.

8. Potter, Wooodburne, *The War in Florida*, Lewis and Coleman, Baltimore: 1836, p. 11.

9. Ott, Eloise R., "Fort King: A Brief History," FHQ, Vol. XLVI, No. 1, July 1967, p. 29.

10. When the Indians won an engagement, the whites generally called it a massacre; when the whites won, it was called a battle.

CHAPTER II

1. Drew, Frank, "Notes on the Origin of the Seminole Indians of Florida," FHQ, Vol. VI, No. 1, July 1927, p. 21.

2. Mahon, John K., *History of the Second Seminole War, 1835–1842*, University of Florida Press, Gainesville, Florida: 1967, p. 8.

3. Porter, Kenneth Wiggins, "The Founder of the Seminole Nation, Secofee or Cowcatcher," FHQ, Vol. XXVII, No. 4, April 1949, p. 362.

4. Mahon, p. 5.

5. Upper Creek warriors whose designation was derived from the war symbol they carried.

6. Bartram, William (Harper, Francis, ed.), *The Travels of William Bartram*, Yale University Press, New Haven, Connecticut: 1958, p. 122.

7. Mahon, p. 6.

8. Bartram, p. 134.

CHAPTER III

1. Anderson, Robert L., "The End of an Idyll," FHQ, Vol. XLII, No. 2, July 1963, p. 35.

2. Ibid.

3. Porter, "Negroes and the Seminole War, 1835–1842," *The Journal of Southern History*, Vol. XXX, No. 4, November 1964, p. 427.

4. Ibid., p. 430.

CHAPTER IV

1. Porter, "Chief Bowlegs," FHQ, Vol. XLV, No. 3, July 1967, p. 219. Bowlegs of the original Cowkeeper dynasty was an uncle of Billy Bowlegs and Micanopy.

2. Mahon, p. 121.

CHAPTER V

1. Chandler, Captain William, Letter of May 17, 1866, quoted in FHQ, Vol. VIII, No. 4, April 1930, p. 197.

2. Mahon, p. 130.

3. Tappan, John S., "Tallahassee and St. Marks in 1841," FHQ, Vol. XXIV, No. 2, October 1945, p. 108.

4. Ibid., p. 110. It is said, however, to have been much exaggerated.

5. Dodd, Dorothy, "Captain Bunce's Tampa Bay Fisheries, 1835–1840," FHQ, Vol. XXV, No. 3, January 1947, p. 246.

CHAPTER VI

1. Glenn, Joshua Nichols, "The Diary of Joshua Nichols Glenn," FHQ, Vol. XXIV, No. 1, October 1945, pp. 121–161.

CHAPTER VII

1. Covington, James W., "Life at Fort Brooke, 1824–1836," FHQ, Vol. XXXVI, No. 4, April 1958. See also his "The Establishment of Fort Brooke," FHQ, Vol. XXI, No. 4, April 1953.

CHAPTER VIII

1. Former Superintendent of Indian Affairs in the War Department.

2. These words were later attributed to General William T. Sherman. Actually he was misquoted, although his subsequent actions belie this.

3. Mahon, p. 77.

4. Ibid., p. 84.

5. Cohen, Myer M., *Notices of Florida and the Campaigns by M. M. Cohen (an officer of the left wing)*, Charleston, S.C., Burges and Honour; New York, B. B. Hussey, 1836; Reprint, University of Florida Press, Gainesville, Florida: 1964, pp. 57–58.

CHAPTER IX

1. Mahon, p. 93.

2. Doctor McLemore was later commissioned a major.

CHAPTER X

1. Bemrose, John, *Reminiscences of the Second Seminole War*, University of Florida Press, Gainesville, Florida: 1966, p. 43.

2. Bittle, George C., "The Florida Militia's Role in the Battle of Withlacoochee," FHQ, Vol. XLIV, No. 4, April 1966, p. 303.

3. Clinch to Adjutant General, January 4, 1836, National Archives.

4. Mahon, p. 110.

CHAPTER XI

1. Private Joseph, who hid in the pond, arrived at Fort Brooke two days later. He subsequently died of his wounds.

2. The United States Revenue Cutter Service was later renamed the United States Coast Guard. Under date of January 6, 1836, Secretary of the Treasury Levi Woodbury placed the *Washington* under the command of the navy.

3. For whom the Transportation Corps' Fort Eustis, near Norfolk, Virginia, was later named.

4. Mahon, p. 152. A similar incident occurred during World War II, with about the same results. During the horrible winter before Cassino, when morale was at a low ebb, a Special Service officer arranged a band concert on the side of Mount Sammucro, in full view of the enemy. With the sun glinting on the snow and the instruments, the band presented a pretty sight. The musicians were hardly into their first piece when the Germans opened up with everything they had. Instruments went one way and the bandsmen and audience the other. The Germans must have thought they had seen everything.

CHAPTER XII

1. Call to Secretary of War, April 30, 1836; to President, May 12, 1836, National Archives.

2. Motte, pp. 227–228.

3. Mahon, p. 185.

CHAPTER XIII

1. Mahon, p. 193.

2. Hollingsworth, Henry (Stanley F. Horn, ed.), " 'Tennessee Volunteers' in the Seminole Campaign: The Diary of Henry Hollingsworth," Tennessee Historical Quarterly, September–December 1942 and March, June, and September 1943, p. 236.

3. Motte, p. 199.

4. Ibid., p. 91.

5. St. Augustine, Florida, *Herald*, November 24, 1836, quoted in Mahon, p. 189.

6. Heinl, Colonel Robert Debs, Jr., USMC, *Soldiers of the Sea*, U.S. Naval Institute, Annapolis, Maryland: 1962, p. 40.

7. There are two Big Cypress Swamps in Florida. The larger is south of Lake Okeechobee.

8. Motte, p. 119.

CHAPTER XIV

1. Mahon, p. 204.

2. Ibid., p. 225.

3. Porter, "Seminole Flight from Fort Marion," FHQ, Vol. XXII, No. 3, January 1944, p. 112.

4. Motte, p. 166.

5. Jesup to Secretary of War, October 22, 1837, National Archives. See also Mahon, p. 215.

6. Jarvis, p. 277.

7. Boyd.

8. Ward, Mary McNeer, "The Disappearance of the Head of Osceola," FHQ, Vol. XXXIII, Nos. 3 and 4, January–April 1955, p. 193. Mrs. Ward was a great-granddaughter of Dr. Weedon.

CHAPTER XV

1. Taylor to Jesup, January 4, 1838, and Buchanan, Lieutenant Robert C. (Frank F. White, ed.), "A Journal of Lt. Robert C.

Buchanan During the Seminole War," FHQ, Vol. XXIX, No. 2, October 1950, p. 132.

2. Motte, p. 182.

3. Ibid., p. 193.

4. Ibid., p. 199.

5. Ibid., p. 210.

CHAPTER XVI

1. This was during the buildup of the army following the Chesapeake-Leopard incident in 1807.

2. Fifty-four Indian and Negro émigrés died on the trip west, Philip among them.

CHAPTER XVII

1. Sprague, Lieutenant John T. (Frank F. White, ed.), "Macomb's Mission to the Seminoles," FHQ, Vol. XXXV, No. 2, October 1956, p. 144.

2. Ibid., p. 178.

3. Ibid., p. 172.

CHAPTER XVIII

1. Covington, "Cuban Bloodhounds and the Seminoles," FHQ, Vol. XXXIII, No. 2, October 1954, p. 111. Most of my information on the bloodhound experiment comes from this superb article.

2. March 17, 1840.

CHAPTER XIX

1. Mahon, p. 303.

2. Cullum's *Biographical Directory of Graduates of the United States Military Academy* notes that Armistead was appointed to West Point because of good behavior as an orderly sergeant at the Battle of Fallen Timbers, August 20, 1794, but Mahon comments (on page 274) that

"If this were true, he would have been nine years old when he took part in that historic fight."

3. St. Augustine, Florida, *Herald*, May 29, 1840.

4. Walker, Hester Perrine, "Massacre at Indian Key, August 7, 1840, and the Death of Doctor Henry Perrine," FHQ, Vol. V, No. 1, July 1926, p. 18. Mrs. Walker was a daughter of Dr. Perrine.

5. Mahon, p. 283.

6. Sprague, *The Origin, Progress and Conclusion of the Florida War*, University of Florida Press, Gainesville, Florida: 1964, pp. 258–260.

CHAPTER XX

1. Mahon, p. 303.

2. Sprague, *The Origin, Progress and Conclusion of the Florida War*, p. 268.

3. Ibid., p. 274.

4. Ibid., pp. 468–469.

5. Worth to Adjutant General, June 14, 1842, National Archives.

6. Vose to Adjutant General, September 26, 1842, National Archives.

7. Mahon, p. 317.

8. Sprague, *The Origin, Progress and Conclusion of the Florida War*, p. 499.

9. There is some question as to when Tiger Tail died. Some evidence indicates that he did not die in New Orleans, but rather continued west and then went with Wildcat's expedition to Mexico, subsequently returning to Florida. There is no doubt that an Indian named Tiger Tail was living near Miami in the 1870s. The death of this Tiger Tail at the age of ninety was reported from Miami in September 1881. See also Porter, "Tiger Tail," FHQ, Vol. XXIV, No. 3, January 1946, p. 216.

Bibliography

BOOKS

Ballentine, George (ed.), *Autobiography of an English Soldier in the United States Army*, New York: 1853.

Bartram, William (Francis Harper, ed.), *The Travels of William Bartram*, Yale University Press, New Haven, Conn.: 1958.

Bemrose, John (John K. Mahon, ed.), *Reminiscences of the Second Seminole War*, University of Florida Press, Gainesville, Florida: 1966.

Blassingame, Wyatt, *Seminoles of Florida*, Department of Agriculture, Tallahassee, Florida: 1959.

Bogges, F. C. M., *A Veteran of Four Wars* (privately printed), Arcadia, Florida: 1900.

Boyd, Mark F., *Florida Aflame*, Florida Historical Quarterly, Tallahassee, Florida: 1951. Reprinted from FHQ, Vol. XXX, No. 1, July 1951.

Brown, G. M., *Ponce de Leon Land and Florida War Record* (privately printed), St. Augustine, Florida: 1902.

Buckmaster, Henrietta, *The Seminole Wars*, Collier Books, New York: 1966.

Clay, C. M., *Speech in the House of Representatives of Kentucky* (privately printed), Frankfort, Kentucky: January 1841.

249

Cohen, M. M., *Notices of Florida and the Campaigns,* University of Florida Press, Gainesville, Florida: 1964.

Conrad, Hair, et al., *Memorial of the Cherokee Mediators,* Government Printing Office, Washington, D.C.: March 26, 1838.

Cooke, David C., *Indians on the Warpath,* Dodd, Mead and Company, New York: 1957.

Cubberly, Frederick, *The Dade Massacre,* Government Printing Office, Washington, D.C.: 1921.

Dunsing, Dee, *War Chant,* Longman's, Green and Co., New York: 1954.

Elderkin, James D., *Biographical Sketches and Anecdotes of a Soldier of Three Wars* (privately printed), Detroit, Michigan: 1899.

Emerson, William C., *The Seminoles: Dwellers of the Everglades,* Exposition Press, New York: 1954.

Evans, Stephen H., *The United States Coast Guard,* The United States Naval Institute, Annapolis, Maryland: 1949.

Foster, Laurence, *Negro-Indian Relationships in the Southeast* (privately printed), Philadelphia: 1935.

Fry, James Barnet, *The History and Legal Effects of Brevets in the Armies of Great Britain and the United States,* D. Van Nostrand, New York: 1877.

Gentry, Major William Richard, Jr., *Full Justice* (privately printed), St. Louis, Missouri: 1937.

Giddings, Joshua R., *Speech in the House of Representatives,* Government Printing Office, Washington, D.C.: February 9, 1841.

———, *The Exiles of Florida* (Quadricentennial Edition), University of Florida Press, Gainesville, Florida: 1964.

Halbe, James M., *Tales of the Seminole War,* The Okeechobee News, Okeechobee, Florida: 1950.

Hall, Gordon Langley, *Osceola,* Holt, Rinehart and Winston, New York: 1964.

Hammersly, L. R., *Records of Living Officers of the United States Army*, L. R. Hammersly and Company, Philadelphia: 1884.

Hanna, A. J., *Fort Maitland*, Fort Maitland Committee, Fort Maitland, Florida: 1936.

Heinl, Robert Debs, *Soldiers of the Sea*, United States Naval Institute, Annapolis, Maryland: 1962.

Laumer, Frank, *Massacre*, University of Florida Press, Gainesville, Florida: 1968.

Lieutenant of the Left Wing, *Sketch of the Seminole War*, D. J. Dowling, Charleston, S. C.: 1836.

Mahon, John K., *History of the Second Seminole War, 1835–1845*, University of Florida Press, Gainesville, Florida: 1967.

Malone, Dumas (ed.), *Dictionary of American Biography*, Vol. VII, Charles Scribner's Sons, New York: 1934.

McCall, Major General George A., *Letters from the Frontier*, J. B. Lippincott and Company, Philadelphia: 1868.

Motte, Jacob Rhett (James F. Sunderman, ed.), *Journey into Wilderness*, University of Florida Press, Gainesville, Florida: 1953.

Munroe, Kirk, *Through Swamp and Glade*, Charles Scribner's Sons, New York: 1896.

Poinsett, Joel R., *Report from Secretary of War*, Government Printing Office, Washington, D.C.: February 21, 1838.

————, *Seminole Indians—Prisoners of War, Letter from Secretary of War*, Government Printing Office, Washington, D.C.: April 11, 1838.

Potter, Woodburne, *The War in Florida*, Baltimore: 1836. Reprint, University Micro-Films, Inc., Lewis and Coleman, Ann Arbor, Michigan: 1966.

Powell, William H., *List of Officers of the U.S. Army 1776–1900*, L. R. Hamersly and Company, New York: 1900.

Pratt, Theodore, *Seminole*, University of Florida Press, Gainesville, Florida: 1953.

Records of Movements, Vessels of the United States Coast Guard, 1790–1933, Office of Assistant Commandant, U.S. Coast Guard, Washington, D.C.: 1934.

Smith, Captain H. D., *Early History of the U.S. Revenue Marine,* Naval Historical Foundation, Washington, D.C.: 1932.

Smith, W. W., *Sketch of the Seminole War,* D. J. Dowling, Charleston, S.C.: 1836.

Solano, Matthew, *Documents Respecting Capt. Sprague's Book,* Government Printing Office, Washington, D.C.: September 1848.

Sprague, John T., *The Origin, Progress and Conclusion of the Florida War,* University of Florida Press, Gainesville, Florida: 1964.

U.S. Army, *Proceedings of a Court of Inquiry in the Case of Major General Scott and Major General Gaines,* Government Printing Office, Washington, D.C.: March 3, 1837.

Walton, George, *The Tarnished Shield,* Dodd, Mead and Company, New York: 1973.

Whitney, Thomas B., *The Ambuscade (An Historical Poem),* J. S. Redfield, Clinton Hall, New York: 1845.

Williams, John Lee, *The Territory of Florida,* 1837.

Wilson, James Grant, and Fiske, John (ed.), *Appleton's Cyclopaedia of American Biography,* Vol. II, D. Appleton and Company, New York: 1898.

ARTICLES

(*Florida Historical Quarterly is herein designated as FHQ*)

Anderson, Robert L., "The End of an Idyll," FHQ, Vol. XLII, No. 2, July 1963, p. 35.

Anon., "Indian Murders," FHQ, Vol. VIII, No. 4, April 1940, p. 200.

Anon., "Miami in 1843," FHQ, Vol. III, No. 3, January 1925, p. 34.

Anon., "Osceola and the Charlestonians," FHQ, Vol. XXXIII, Nos. 3 and 4, January–April 1955, p. 247.

Anon., "Old Tiger Tail Dead," FHQ, Vol. IV, No. 4, April 1926, p. 192.

Anon., "The White Flag," FHQ, Vol. XXXIII, Nos. 3 and 4, January–April 1955, p. 218.

Bittle, George C., "First Campaign of the Second Seminole War," FHQ, Vol. XLVI, No. 1, July 1967, p. 39.

————, "The Florida Militia's Role in the Battle of Withlacoochee," FHQ, Vol. XLIV, No. 4, April 1966, p. 303.

Boyd, Mark F., "Asi-Ya Holo or Osceola," FHQ, Vol. XXXIII, Nos. 3 and 4, January–April 1955, p. 249.

————, "Osceola and the Charlestonians," FHQ, Vol. XXXIII, Nos. 3 and 4, January–April 1955, p. 247.

————, "The Seminole War: Its Background and Onset," FHQ, Vol. XXX, No. 1, July 1951, p. 2.

Brevard, Caroline Mays, "Richard Keith Call," FHQ, Vol. I, No. 2, July 1908, p. 3.

————, "Richard Keith Call," FHQ, Vol. I, No. 3, October 1908, p. 8.

Buchanan, Lieutenant Robert C. (Frank F. White, ed.), "A Journal of Lt. Robert C. Buchanan During the Seminole War," FHQ, Vol. XXIX, No. 2, October 1950, p. 132.

Buker, George E., "Lieutenant Levin M. Powell, USN, Pioneer of Riverine Warfare," FHQ, Vol. XLVII, No. 3, January 1969, p. 253.

Cass, Lewis, "To the Public" (privately printed), Paris, March 6, 1837.

Chandler, Captain William, Letter, FHQ, Vol. VIII, No. 4, April 1930, p. 197.

————, "A Tallahassee Alarm of 1836," FHQ, Vol. VIII, No. 4, April 1930, p. 197.

Cobb, Samuel E., "The Florida Militia and the Affair at Withlacoochee," FHQ, Vol. XIX, No. 2, October 1940, p. 128.

Coe, Charles H., "The Parentage and Birthplace of Osceola," FHQ, Vol. XVII, No. 4, April 1939, p. 304.

————, "The Parentage of Osceola," FHQ, Vol. XXXIII, Nos. 3 and 4, January–April 1955, p. 202.

Covington, James W., "Cuban Bloodhounds and the Seminoles," FHQ, Vol. XXXIII, No. 2, October 1954, p. 111.

————, "Federal Relations with the Apalachicola Indians, 1823–1838," FHQ, Vol. XLII, No. 2, October 1963, p. 125.

————, "Life at Fort Brooke 1824–1836," FHQ, Vol. XXXVI, No. 4, April 1958, p. 319.

————, "Migration of the Seminoles into Florida 1700–1820," FHQ, Vol. XLVI, No. 4, April 1968, p. 340.

———— (ed.), "The Establishment of Fort Brooke," FHQ, Vol. XXXI, No. 4, April 1953, p. 271.

Davis, T. Frederick, "Pioneer Florida," FHQ, No. 2, October 1943, p. 57.

————, "The Seminole Council, October 23–25, 1834," FHQ, Vol. VII, No. 4, April 1929, p. 330.

Dodd, Dorothy, "Captain Bunce's Tampa Bay Fisheries, 1835–1840," FHQ, Vol. XXV, No. 3, January 1947, p. 246.

Doherty, Herbert J., "Richard K. Call vs. the Federal Government on the Seminole War," FHQ, Vol. XXXI, No. 3, January 1953, p. 163.

Donaldson, Thomas, "The George Catlin Indian Gallery in the U.S. National Museum" (Catlin Notes), *Annual Report of the Regents of the Smithsonian Institution*, Government Printing Office, Washington, D.C.: 1885.

Eby, Cecil D., Jr., "Memoir of a West Pointer in Florida, 1825," FHQ, Vol. XLI, No. 2, October 1962, p. 154.

Forry, Samuel, Letters, FHQ, Vol. VI, No. 3, January 1928, p. 133.

———, Letters, FHQ, Vol. VI, No. 4, April 1928, p. 206.

Glenn, Joshua Nichols, "The Diary of Joshua Nichols Glenn," FHQ, Vol. XXIV, No. 1, October 1945, pp. 121–161.

Goggin, John M., "Osceola: Portraits, Features, and Dress," FHQ, Vol. XXXIII, Nos. 3 and 4, January–April 1955.

———, "The Seminole Negroes of Andros Island, Bahamas," FHQ, Vol. XXIV, No. 3, January 1946, p. 201.

Griffin, John W., "The Addison Blockhouse," FHQ, Vol. XXX, No. 3, January 1952, p. 286.

Hammond, E. A., "Bemrose's Medical Case Notes from the Second Seminole War," FHQ, Vol. XLVII, No. 4, April 1969, p. 401.

Hollingsworth, Henry (Stanley F. Horn, ed.), " 'Tennessee Volunteers' in the Seminole Campaign: The Diary of Henry Hollingsworth," *Tennessee Historical Quarterly*, September–December 1942, March, June–September 1943, p. 236.

Howe, Charles, "A Letter from Indian Key, 1840," FHQ, Vol. XX, No. 2, October 1941, p. 197.

Hoyt, William D., Jr., "A Soldier's View of the Seminole War 1838–1839," FHQ, Vol. XXV, No. 4, April 1947, p. 356.

Jarvis, Nathan S., "An Army Surgeon's Notes on Frontier Service, 1833–1848," *Journal of the Military Service of the United States*, September–October, 1906.

Laumer, Frank, "Encounter by the River," FHQ, Vol. XLVI, No. 4, April 1968, p. 322.

———, "This Was Fort Dade," FHQ, Vol. XLV, No. 1, January 1966, p. 1.

Mahon, John K., "Letters from the Second Seminole War," FHQ, Vol. XXXVI, No. 4, April 1958, p. 331.

———, "Postscript to John Bemrose's Reminiscences," FHQ, Vol. XLVII, No. 1, July 1968, p. 59.

————, "The Treaty of Moultrie Creek, 1823," FHQ, Vol. XXXX, No. 4, April 1962, p. 350.

Martin, Sidney Walter, "Richard Keith Call, Florida Territorial Leader," FHQ, Vol. XXI, No. 4, April 1943, p. 332.

Moore, John Hammond, "A South Carolina Lawyer Visits St. Augustine, 1837," FHQ, Vol. XLII, No. 4, April 1965, p. 361.

Moore-Wilson, Minne, "The Seminole Indians of Florida," FHQ, Vol. VII, No. 1, July 1928, p. 75.

Muncey, Albert C., "Some Military Affairs in Territorial Florida," FHQ, Vol. XXV, No. 2, October 1946, p. 202.

Neill, Wilfred T., "The Site of Osceola's Village in Marion County, Florida," FHQ, Vol. XXXIII, Nos. 3 and 4, January–April 1955, p. 240.

Ott, E. R., 'Ocala Prior to 1868," FHQ, Vol. VI, No. 2, October 27, 1927, p. 85.

Ott, Eloise R., "Fort King: A Brief History," FHQ, Vol. XLVI, No. 1, July 1967, p. 29.

Palmer, Sarah R. W., "Henry Perrine—Pioneer, Botanist, and Horticulturalist," FHQ, Vol. V, No. 2, October 1926, p. 112.

Pasco, Samuel, "Jefferson County, Florida, 1827–1910," FHQ, Vol. VII, No. 3, January 1929, p. 234.

Phelps, Lieutenant John W., Letters, FHQ, Vol. VI, No. 2, October 1927, p. 85.

Porter, Kenneth Wiggins, "Billy Bowlegs (Holata Micco) in the Seminole Wars," FHQ, Vol. XLV, No. 3, January 1967, p. 219.

————, "The Cowkeeper Dynasty of the Seminole Nation," FHQ, Vol. XXX, No. 4, April 1952, p. 341.

————, "The Episode of Osceola's Wife, Fact or Fiction," FHQ, Vol. XXVI, No. 1, July 1947, p. 92.

————, "The Founder of the 'Seminole Nation,' Secoffee or Cowkeeper," FHQ, Vol. XXVII, No. 4, April 1949, p. 362.

————, "Jacksonville and the Seminole War, 1835–1836," FHQ, Vol. III, No. 3, January 1925, p. 10, No. 4, April 1925, p. 15, Vol. IV, No. 1, July 1925, p. 22.

————, "John Caesar: Seminole Negro Partisan," *Journal of Negro History*, Vol. XXX, 1946, p. 190.

————, "The Negro Abraham," FHQ, Vol. XXV, No. 1, July 1946, p. 1.

————, "Negroes and the Seminole War, 1835–1842," *The Journal of Southern History*, Vol. XXX, No. 4, November 1964, p. 427.

————, "Notes on Seminole Negroes in the Bahamas," FHQ, Vol. XXIV, No. 1, July 1945, p. 56.

————, "Osceola and the Negroes," FHQ, Vol. XXXIII, Nos. 3 and 4, January–April 1955, p. 235.

————, "Seminole Flight from Fort Marion," FHQ, Vol. XXII, No. 3, January 1944, p. 112.

————, "Tiger Tail," FHQ, Vol. XXIV, No. 3, January 1946, p. 216.

Reasons, George, and Patrick, Sam, "Abraham—Key Seminole War Figure," Weekender, Washington *Star*, January 30, 1971.

Roberts, Albert Hubbard, "The Dade Massacre," FHQ, Vol. V, No. 3, January 1927, p. 123.

Scott, Kenneth, "The City of Wreckers," FHQ, Vol. XXV, No. 2, October 1946, p. 191.

Sheldon, Jane Murrey, "Seminole Attacks near New Smyrna," New Smyrna *Breeze*, 1890; FHQ, Vol. VIII, No. 3, January 1930, p. 188.

Sprague, John T. (Frank F. White, ed.), "Macomb's Mission to the Seminoles," FHQ, Vol. XXXV, No. 2, October 1956, p. 142.

Stafford, Robert Charles, "The Bemrose Manuscript on the Seminole War," FHQ, Vol. LXVIII, No. 4, April 1940.

Sturtevant, William O., "Notes on Modern Seminole Traditions of Osceola," FHQ, Vol. XXXIII, Nos. 3 and 4, January–April 1955, p. 206.

———, "Osceola's Coats?" FHQ, Vol. XXXIV, No. 4, April 1956, p. 315.

Tanner, Earl C., "The Early Career of Edwin T. Jenckes," FHQ, Vol. XXX, No. 3, January 1952, p. 261.

Tappan, John S., "Tallahassee and St. Marks in 1841," FHQ, Vol. XXIV, No. 2, October 1945, p. 108.

Waldo, Horatio, "Richard K. Call—Thomas Brown," Florida Journal, March 17, 1841; FHQ, Vol. VI, No. 3, January 1928, p. 156.

Walker, Hester Perrine, "Massacre at Indian Key, August 7, 1840, and the Death of Doctor Henry Perrine," FHQ, Vol. V, No. 1, July 1926, p. 18.

Ward, Mary McNeer, "The Disappearance of the Head of Osceola," FHQ, Vol. XXXIII, Nos. 3 and 4, January and April 1955, p. 193.

Weidenbach, Nell L., "Lieutenant John T. McLaughlin: Guilty or Innocent?" FHQ, Vol. XLVI, No. 1, July 1967, p. 46.

White, Frank F., Jr., "Scouting Expedition Along Lake Panasoffkee," FHQ, Vol. XXXI, No. 4, April 1953, p. 282.

——— (ed.), "A Journal of Lt. Robert C. Buchanan During the Seminole War (The Battle of Okeechobee)," FHQ, Vol. XXIX, No. 2, October 1950, p. 132.

———, "The Journals of Lieutenant John Pickell, 1836–1837," FHQ, Vol. XXXVIII, No. 2, October 1959, p. 142.

———, "Macomb's Mission to the Seminoles," FHQ, Vol. XXXV, No. 2, October 1956, p. 130.

Wik, Reynold M., "Captain Nathaniel Wyche Hunter and the Florida Indian Campaigns, 1837–1841," FHQ, Vol. XXXIX, No. 1, July 1960, p. 62.

Williams, Ernest L., Jr., "Negro Slavery in Florida," FHQ, Vol. XXVIII, No. 1, July 1949, p. 98.

Williams, Isabella M., "The Truth Concerning Tiger-Tail," FHQ, Vol. IV, No. 2, October 1925, p. 68.

Winder, C. H., "A Card," *National Intelligencer*, March 8, 1844, Library of Congress.

Woodward, A. L., "Indian Massacre in Gadsden County," FHQ, Vol. I, No. 1, April 1908, p. 17.

Young, Capt. Hugh, "The Memoir," FHQ, Vol. XIII, No. 1, July 1934, p. 20.

Young, Rogers W., "Fort Marion During the Seminole War, 1835–1842," FHQ, Vol. XIII, No. 4, April 1935, p. 193.

GOVERNMENT DOCUMENTS

Assistant Adjutant General, Department of the South, *Record of Officers and Soldiers Killed*, GPO, Washington, D.C.: 1882; Library of Congress.

Cubberly, Frederick, *The Dade Massacre*, GPO, Washington, D.C.: 1921; House of Representatives, Library of Congress.

Memorial of the Cherokee Mediators, GPO, Washington, D.C.: March 26, 1838; Library of Congress.

Secretary of War, *Documents, Captain Sprague's Book, Seminole War*, GPO, Washington, D.C.: September 15, 1848; Library of Congress.

Secretary of War, *Letter*, April 11, 1838, GPO, Washington, D.C., Library of Congress.

Secretary of War, *Report*, February 21, 1838, GPO, Washington, D.C., Library of Congress.

War Department, *Estimate of Appropriation—Indian Hostilities*, GPO, Washington, D.C.: March 21, 1838; Library of Congress.

MANUSCRIPT

McClellan, Major Edward North, *History of the United States Marine Corps*, Vol. 2, Part One, Marine Corps Historical Library, Arlington, Virginia: 1930.

PUBLIC RECORDS

Letters in and out, Office of Secretary of War, 1835–1842, National Archives.

Records of the Adjutant General, 1835–1842, National Archives.

LIBRARIES CONSULTED

Alexandria Public Library, Alexandria, Virginia.

Coast Guard Library, Washington, D.C.

Library of Congress, Washington, D.C.

Marine Corps Historical Library, Arlington, Virginia.

National Archives Library, Washington, D.C.

University of Florida Library, Gainesville, Florida.

Cedar Key, Florida, Branch of the Central Florida Regional Library, Ocala.

Florida Atlantic University Library, Boca Raton, Florida.

Boca Raton Public Library, Boca Raton, Florida.

Georgia Southern College Library, Statesboro, Georgia.

Index

261

population of, 49, 51–52,
211–12
Spanish settlement of, 20, 21,
25, 26, 38, 43, 51, 52, 53
as training ground for future
wars, 239
U.S. raids into, 39
white settlers in, 78–79, 82,
89, 128, 151, 152, 167–68,
181, 189, 193–94, 201,
204, 211, 221, 227, 232
Florida (U.S. army transport), 66
Florida Militia, 89–91, 116, 118,
129, 132, 133, 135, 136,
148, 150, 154, 155, 189,
193–94, 219
Florida Volunteers, 94, 173
Fort Alabama, 116, 119, 148. *See
also* Fort Foster
Fort Armstrong, 148
Fort Bessinger, 175
Fort Brooke, 1, 2, 3, 4, 12, 13,
15, 18, 52, 66–67, 77, 101,
102, 107, 109, 113, 116,
117, 143, 177, 219, 229
Fort Christmas, 178
Fort Clinch, 148
Fort Cummings, 222
Fort Dade, 148, 189
Fort Dallas, 220, 221
Fort Drane, 12, 94, 107, 109,
112, 113, 119, 126, 127–
28, 129, 133, 134, 148
Fort Floyd, 178
Fort Foster, 148
Fort Frazer, 175
Fort Gardner, 175, 177
Fort Gibson, 191

Treaty of, 11*n*, 83–85
Fort Gibson Indian Territory,
33
Fort Heilman, 219
Fort Izard, 110, 111, 112, 113,
123
Fort Jupiter, 180, 181
Fort King, 2, 4, 10, 11, 12, 13,
15, 77, 93, 109, 126, 198,
211, 214, 219
Fort Lauderdale, 178, 183
Fort Marion, 159–60, 172
Fort Mellon, 172, 193, 204
Fort Micanopy, 221
Fort Moosa, 28
Fort Negro, 32, 41
Fort Payton, 155
Fort Pierce, 178, 228
Fort Scott, 41, 42, 62*n*
Fort Wacahoota, 221
Fort Weadman, 214, 215
Foster (U.S. lieutenant colonel),
150, 151
Fourth Artillery, 77, 183
Fourth Infantry, 1, 2, 77, 174,
176, 177, 232
Fowltown, 41, 42
Francis, Joseph, 32, 43
Fuche Loste Hadjo (Seminole
Chief), 72
Fulton, William F., 179
Fuse Hadjo (Seminole Chief),
235

Gadsden, James, 61, 63, 65, 66,
79–80, 81
Gaines, Edmund Pendleton, 41,
42, 43, 46, 62*n*, 103, 105,
112, 191